Have a Great Day
Every Day!

• *Meditations for Growing Christians* •

Have a Great Day Every Day!

Arthur G. McPhee

HERALD PRESS
Scottdale, Pennsylvania
Kitchener, Ontario
1984

Library of Congress Cataloging in Publication Data

McPhee, Arthur, 1945-
 Have a great day every day!

 1. Devotional calendars. I. Title.
 BV4811.M36   1984   242'.2   84-565
 ISBN 0-8361-3352-8 (pbk.)

HAVE A GREAT DAY EVERY DAY!
Copyright © 1984 by Herald Press, Scottdale, Pa. 15683
 Published simultaneously in Canada by Herald Press,
 Kitchener, Ont. N2G 4M5. All rights reserved.
Library of Congress Catalog Card Number: 84-565
International Standard Book Number: 0-8361-3352-8
Printed in the United States of America
Design by Ann Graber
84 85 86 87 88 89 12 11 10 9 8 7 6 5 4 3 2 1

For Bobby

Contents

WEEK 3

Learn the Joy of Loving Others

WEEK 4

Cultivate Your Friendships

WEEK 5

Get Your Priorities in Order

WEEK 6

Overcome the Tyranny of the Urgent

WEEK 7

Get to Know God Better

WEEK 8

Learn the Habit of Daily Prayer

Author's Preface

"Oh, no! Not you too!" said my friend when I told her about this book. My friend is weary of seeing exclamation point books on the shelves of her favorite bookshop. "Can anyone seriously suggest that it's possible to have a great day every day?" she asked.

However, I decided to retain the title despite my friend's protest—but not for any of the following reasons: (1) to raise false hopes by promising days without troubles; (2) to suggest that everyone become a Pollyanna; (3) to promote escapism; or (4) to get attention. Having twisted my ankle and sprained my knee today, I know that life is not devoid of pain; having put on false fronts and hating myself for it, I know that Pollyannas often feel dishonest on the inside; having run away from problems-a-plenty, I know that running away from troubles is the surest way to multiply them; and having gotten enough attention to have a few thousand new expectations and responsibilities thrust at me, I can certainly do without vying to become the next Rabbi Norman Vincent Sheen.

But I have also experienced the joy of following Christ daily in life—of seeing him change depressing circumstances into hope, hearing him speak just the note of cheer or word of guidance I needed, and feeling him

11

strengthen me the moment I despaired of my weakness. I have known his help to change attitudes, his love to build friendships, his will to get my life under control. So, it is difficult not to be enthusiastic.

I do not need to ask God for his ID card. He has made himself known to me daily by putting enough joy and purpose and surprise into my life to turn even some of the worst days into great ones!

E. Stanley Jones used to say the art of living is the least well learned of all arts, and that while we have learned the art of existing, of getting along, of making it from day to day, few of us have come close at all to getting the most out of life.

For a long time that described me, too. I was going through the motions without ever getting into the act of living. Unfortunately, it's still that way at times, but I've been making regular, even if not spectacular, progress. I've been encouraged enough by that process, in fact, to offer eight principles that have been of help. By faithfully applying them, I'm convinced you, too, can move beyond merely existing to real living.

But there's also a ninth principle, which I've woven into the very fabric of this book, as it needs to be woven into the fabric of our lives. It is the principle of framing each day with times for prayer, study, and self-examination.

Many have been in the habit of beginning each day with God, but it's equally beneficial to finish the day with him. I've learned that searching out the lessons of each day before I go to bed is just as valuable as thinking about what's ahead when I get up in the morning.

So, you'll notice as you begin, this book is not meant to be read straight through. It is designed, not only to acquaint you with eight valuable insights for experiencing life at its best, but to give you help in forming a pattern of letting God guide you. For 56 days you will set aside time at the beginning of the day for study and conversation with God. You will open the door on that day's opportunities and step over the threshhold with Him at your side. But for 56 days you will also set aside time in the evening to summarize the day: to pull everything together; to figure out how all the pieces fit; to rejoice in what has gone well, and to straighten out what has gone awry; to pray for those with whom you've crossed paths; to pray for yourself that you may learn well the lessons of the day; and to get something of the long view, reflecting on how your day fits into God's total plan for your life.

In this way, you will not only discover another secret of getting the most out of every day, but you'll come to appreciate more deeply Jesus' wonderful gift of access into the very throne room of the Father.

Start the day with God . . . finish the day with God. That's the key to getting out of bed in the morning, raising the shades to the sunshine (or in the rain!), and exclaiming with the psalmist, "This is the day the Lord has made; let us rejoice and be glad in it!" It is one of the secrets to learning the art of living, to squeezing the best out of every waking moment. Framing the day with God—by it, he prods you to grow, to apply the lessons of the day, and to have a marvelous time in the process.

—*Arthur G. McPhee*
Needham, Massachusetts

Turn Your Troubles into Triumphs

Perspective

"Why are you downcast, Oh my soul? Why so disturbed within me? Put your hope in God, for I will yet praise him, my Savior and my God" (Psalm 42:5).

The first principle to help you move from existing to real living is to turn your troubles into triumphs. The question, "Why are you cast down, Oh my soul?" is one with which all of us identify. It is raised often by the writers of Scripture, especially in the Psalms. This should not surprise us: troubles will come. We cannot escape them.

I heard someone say she has never learned to trust happiness. I can understand that. Even though life may go smoothly for a long time, sooner or later depression or difficulty or disaster comes. The question is not how to avoid trouble. It is what to do with it when it arrives.

What the psalmist did was to talk to himself. He said to his soul, "Why are you so disturbed?" In other words, "Why are you letting the circumstances get you down so?" Then he advised himself, "Put your hope in God."

That must be our approach. Instead of letting feelings take over, rather than being overwhelmed by emotions, we must take charge of ourselves. We must remind ourselves that we are no longer helpless. We have put our trust in God, and God will see us through.

A woman wrote me that her three sons had all been killed as young men—two earlier, and a third in an automobile accident just a few weeks before she wrote me.

"How do I deal with this?" she asked me. I had no glib or easy answer for her, but I was glad to note in her letter that she had not lost her faith. Her heavenly Father also knew the pain of a son's death.

Repeatedly, the Bible reminds us that the afflictions we face can be blessings in disguise if we have the right attitude toward them:

Job 23:10: "But he knows the way that I take; when he has tested me, I will come forth as gold."

2 Corinthians 4:17: "For our light and momentary troubles are achieving for us an eternal glory that far outweighs them all."

1 Peter 4:12: "Dear friends, do not be surprised at the painful trial you are suffering, as though something strange were happening to you."

1 Peter 1:7: "These have come so that your faith—of greater worth than gold, which perishes even though refined by fire—may be proved genuine and may result in praise, glory and honor when Jesus Christ is revealed."

Having a great day every day doesn't mean that all our moments are filled with happiness and no troubles. But it does mean that every moment can be filled with the deep, abiding joy of knowing God. We can face troubles with the confidence that beyond them life can become more full, more rewarding than ever before.

As we shall see, God has a way of turning the worst into good. When we begin to look at life with "the long view," understanding something of the ultimate purposes of God, momentary troubles can be faced with joy. At first frustration, depression, or personal loss may seem overwhelming. But if, like the psalmist, we learn to address ourselves, reminding ourselves of our hope in God, we will find the cloud lifting and the sun breaking through.

Never Let Troubles Get You Down

MORNING

We all know about trouble's negative side, but few of us have given much thought to its potential for good. We view it as a burden, but it also has the potential to lift burdens. It all depends on your perspective—on your way of perceiving it. The old Puritans used to say about illness, for example, that the worst kind of affliction is a dumb one—that is, one that doesn't teach you anything.

Maltbie Babcock reflected: "The tests of life are to make, not break us. Trouble may demolish a man's business, but build up his character. The blow at the outer man may be the greatest blessing to the inner man. If God, then, puts or permits anything hard in our lives, be sure that the real peril, the real trouble, is that we shall lose if we flinch or rebel."°

I am convinced that if everyone had such insight into the beneficial side of trouble, there would be far fewer defeated persons in the world. Somehow, we need to realize, as someone humorously put it, "There may be a last straw that breaks the camel's back, but most of the other straws help develop its muscles." Isn't it sad that so many broken persons haven't realized that?

The Bible says all things work together for good to those who love God. Notice it says "work together." It's not that every trouble's good side can immediately be recognized, or even that it can be seen in retrospect. But in many cases you *can* see the direct benefit. The sum of the burdens we bear in life is the pushing out of our growing edge, helping us to become all God intended us to be when he first thought of us.

EVENING

The old Puritans used to say, "The worst kind of affliction is a dumb one." By that they meant an affliction that doesn't teach you anything. Make a list of all the things that irritated you or troubled you today. What can you learn from each of them?

°Quoted by Gerald Kennedy in *A Second Reader's Notebook* (New York: Harper and Brothers, 1959), p. 30.

Give Your Troubles to God

MORNING

In the play *Alice Through the Looking Glass*, Alice encounters the white knight, who is carrying a beehive. "What are you carrying that for?" she asks. "Well, if I run into a swarm of bees, I can catch them," says the knight. "What about those mouse traps? What are you doing with those?" asks Alice. "Well," the knight responds, "I might run into some mice, too, and I can catch them." "But what about those knives around the feet of your horse?" "Well, I might be crossing some rough waters," said the knight. "And if I run into sharks, the knives on the feet of the horse will ward them off."

Too many of us travel through life like that. But God offers us the joy of knowing we can turn our troubles over to him. Just think of it—we simply come to him, and worry goes, depression goes, anger goes, and life is filled with the health and happiness we want.

Then, why do so few go to God? Why have so few learned the joy of giving their troubles to him? Why, instead, do so many (maybe even you?) assume there's no way to overcome worry and depression and the like?

I suspect it has something to do with the devil clouding our minds with doubts, doing his best to convince us there's no hope.

21

But don't believe it! Do you tend to become depressed? Well, that depression *is* removable. Do you tend to worry? That worry is something you can overcome, too. Do you often get angry? Well, temper, too, can be defused. There is not one form of inner tension that cannot be dissolved when joy fills the heart. Anything that is destructive to your well-being, that tears away at your inner spirit, can be displaced by the joy of knowing God is ready to take all your cares upon himself.

Half of all illnesses, some doctors say, have no organic base at all but are brought on by inner tension. Worry, for instance, can cause ulcers, colitis, heart disease, and even cancer. This is just part of the reason why the joy of knowing that God wants us to cast all our cares on him is vital to living. That knowledge is not a luxury (nor is putting it into practice) but a necessity for those of us who expect to have a great day every day.

EVENING

What are your three biggest worries right now? What would happen if they became God's worries instead of yours? Well, of course, they can become his worries (Matthew 11:29; 1 Peter 5:7). So, take them to him tonight, and ask him for the joy of knowing that everything's under control—his control!

Trade in Satan's Worst for God's Best

MORNING

Of North America's wild flowers, the Lady's Slipper is one of the most exquisite—but also one of the most fragile. It is too delicate for your bouquet or even for transplanting.

The Monarch butterfly is known for the beauty of its patterned wings and the choreography of its flight. But handle a Monarch, and you spoil both the pattern and the flight.

As with the Lady's Slipper and the Monarch, many of the finest things in life are also the most delicate and fragile.

Maybe you know that only too well. Maybe you've already been careless with something precious to you, which you took for granted. Perhaps it was your family, or your chastity, or your integrity, or a friendship. You didn't realize how fragile such treasures were. You wish you had. But now they're gone. It's too late.

The Bible teaches that we have an adversary, the devil, who is out to destroy the most precious—and fragile—thing of all: our very souls. Sometimes we forget there's a kind of civil war going on in the universe, and that Satan is out to use every device he can to spoil the thing that is most precious of all to us and to God.

23

But the Bible also teaches that God has the power to take the devil's worst and turn it into good. He took the greatest minus of history (the cross) and turned it into the greatest plus, and he can work the same miracle in our lives whenever the devil tries to put us on the rack.

The devil has all sorts of means of tearing away at the things that are most precious to us, and sometimes we discover those things are more fragile and delicate than we thought. But whether it's sickness, tragedy, defeat, or disappointment he tries to put on us—even if it's a devious exploitation of our personal weaknesses—God is in control. And in everything, we have the assurance that God works for the good of those who love him. So, when you're in trouble, get in touch with God immediately. And out of the worst, will come the best.

EVENING

Take a few minutes this evening to reflect on how God has delivered you from trouble in the past. Make a list of several instances, especially those where God has brought unexpected good out of total frustration. Thank God for his help, and ask him to help you to think immediately of his availability and willingness to help next time you are in trouble.

Release God's Power Resources Within You

MORNING

Feeling a bit under the weather, I decided to phone Jim rather than visit. "Hi, Jim, how are you?" I said. "Just great," he replied. "Just great!" After the call, I placed the receiver on the cradle and shook my head. Feeling great? I thought. After nearly having been killed?

I knew that Jim must be having a great deal of pain as the result of the injuries he'd received in his near-fatal accident. And that was not all. This accident had been just one in a series of ordeals this young man had been through recently. This was his third brush with death in a year. It sounded strange to hear someone who'd been through all he had say that he felt great.

But I've known others who could face trouble that way. Take Scott, for example. Scott was a teenager who'd fallen from the face of a cliff a thousand miles from home. Knowing absolutely no one in our community, he was forced to remain in traction in the local hospital for weeks. Yet, not once did I hear him complain. Nor did I ever find him in an uncheerful mood.

Or take Jill, a vibrant, vivacious young woman with everything to live for; yet, she learned one day that she had a few months to live at most. However, the knowledge of her impending death did not diminish her cheery demeanor or her radiant character in the slightest. If anything, in fact, she seemed more cheerful.

But it's wrong to assume such persons escape from dealing with anxiety and depression altogether. A well-known clergyman used to say that the man or woman who doesn't find suffering a distressful thing is suffering from either a hardening of the heart or a softening of the brain.

So, Jim, Scott, and Jill were not remarkable because they escaped trauma—be assured, they didn't escape it. Rather, it was the inner resources of strength they laid hold of—inner resources that sprang from their deep faith in Jesus Christ—that enabled them to rise above their circumstances.

EVENING

Like Jim and Scott and Jill, you undoubtedly have Christian friends who have withstood great pressure and stress in time of trouble. Think about one such person you know. What can you learn from how God helped him? How might that have helped you even today?

Always Find Trouble's Positive Side

MORNING

The other day I greeted a friend with a "Hi, Sally, how are you today?" to which she responded, "Oh, pretty well, under the circumstances." So I said to her, "What are you doing under there?" We both laughed, but I'd been partly serious, because there are ways to lift the burdens that weigh us down.

All of us have resources available to face our troubles and not be defeated by them. I have seen too many friends with faces aglow, who had good reason to be in the depths of despair, to doubt it. There are inner resources of strength available to us all, through which we can be overcomers—I am convinced of it!

One of the key differences between those who are overcomers and those who are overcome is in the *perspective* on trouble. Most people regard trouble as something to be avoided at all costs. And if they can't avoid it, they either become bitter and despairing, or they try to deny their trouble by drowning it in drink or fantasies or some so-called "pain killer." But there's another, better way to view trouble: as opportunity—as something which, despite its unpleasantness, can produce good.

Have you ever been swept off your feet and thrown down by the huge waves that roll onto some beaches?

Experience has taught me to hightail it when I see one coming. But a surfer does just the opposite. He paddles his board right out to one of the giants, watching it carefully as it develops. Then, just when the wave reaches up with its watery paw and you think it's going to pound him to the bottom, he gets to his feet and skillfully rides it in to shore! It's a breathless experience even for the spectator! Instead of getting buried by the wave, the surfer uses it to his advantage and turns his experience from something ominous into something beautiful.

The Bible teaches we can face every trouble as the surfer faces the wave. Relying on God as our strength, every trouble has some potential for good. And when seen from God's perspective, that good is sure to come to light.

EVENING

Make a list of the most troublesome things you faced today. With God's help, try to discover a potential bright side to each of those difficulties.

Remind Yourself That Troubles Pass

MORNING

The old man had experienced more than his share of troubles, but through them all he remained radiant. "How come you're always so cheerful?" someone asked. "Well, I'll tell ya," he replied. "I get it outa the Bible. Over and over it says, 'And it came to pass,' but never does it say, 'And it came to stay.' "

We may have trouble with the old man's way of reading the Bible, but it's difficult to find fault with the truth he stated, isn't it? The burdens we face *are* usually temporary. Usually trouble is a temporary thing that gives us grief for the moment, but in the end it strengthens us and equips us with renewed stamina for the greater trials that may come later.

That's why the Bible can say of trouble, "Consider it pure joy . . . whenever you face trials of many kinds, because you know that the testing of your faith develops perseverance. Perseverance must finish its work so that you may be mature and complete, not lacking anything" (James 1:2-4).

Those two perspectives on the difficulties we face in life sum up the difference between those who are trouble's victims and those who have victory over their trouble. But there's an additional perspective on trouble that contributes to the difference, too. That is the realization that troubles are not something you keep to yourself.

In a way that seems obvious. If you're struggling with something and you want encouragement and help, you don't bury your problem and tell no one about it. You share it. You can do so with a friend, in a small group, in a minister's study, with a professional counselor—in many ways.

But there's another way to share trouble. Instead of just unloading burdens for your own benefit, you can share the comfort you've received from God for someone else's benefit—someone who's facing similar difficulties. The Bible calls God "the God of all comfort." When we share the availability of that comfort with others, they can learn for themselves that "he is the God who comforts all."

EVENING

What kinds of things get you down? How many of them are long-term problems and how many of them are short-term? Remind yourself that even the long-term problems have a divine solution, and in the meantime, God will give you strength.

Invest Your Troubles for Good

MORNING

Have you ever received financial help from a friend when you were in a bind, or been encouraged by the story of someone else's overcoming a burden as heavy as your own? Of course, you have. But have you made it a practice to pass on similar help to others who are in trouble?

That's something most of us have never thought much about doing, even though we may have been helped when somebody else has shared with us in our difficulty. One of the women in a church I pastored told how her bouts with depression and her victory over them were proving to be just the background she needed to help a neighbor who was wrestling with despair. The book of Proverbs encourages such an attitude: "Friends always show their love. What are brothers for if not to share trouble?" (17:17, TEV).

Raymond Linquist said that life's greatest waste is not the waste that results from a forest fire or the wasted tons of water that plummet unused over countless waterfalls. He said it is not even the wasted billions that keep us up to our necks in the arms race. Rather, it is "the enormous amount of personal suffering that never gets invested."

There's more than one way to invest trouble, though:

for instance, in letting it sink deep into our minds that there are more important things in the world than physical comfort; or in giving comfort to those who are facing troubles of the same kind we have faced.

Just knowing that our trouble can be invested for good, especially for the good of others—is a kind of strength in itself. That, along with the most basic understanding that trouble always contains a built-in potential for good, is just the strength we need to cope.

EVENING

What struggles has God helped you cope with recently? Who do you know who might be encouraged or comforted by your sharing about how God helped you? Decide tonight to get together with that person as soon as you can in order to invest your troubles for good. In that way you may both see a mediocre day transformed into a great one!

Handle Your Handicaps

Perspective

*"I pray that out of his glorious riches he may
strengthen you with power through his Spirit in your
inner being" (Ephesians 3:16).*

The second principle on the way to having a great day
every day is similar to the first: you must learn to handle
your handicaps.

Troubles are acute, short-lived; handicaps are chronic.
Sometimes handicaps are physical and unavoidable.
More often, however, they are spiritual and attitudinal.
Of the two, spiritual and attitudinal handicaps are the
toughest to handle. Bad habits, chronic guilt feelings, a
lousy self-image, sour grapes, and selfishness often seem
to be tunnels without ends. No matter how hard you grit
your teeth, your vows and resolutions to change come to
nothing. You discover you have no power to carry them
out.

But fortunately that's not the last word. You don't have
the power to leave those sins behind, but the Lord Jesus
Christ does. So, no matter how powerful your resolve to
overcome some fault, never rely on it. Build only on Jesus
Christ and his ability. Set aside all your resolutions except
one—dependence upon him.

Like David, lift your eyes to the hills (in other words, to
the Lord) for help. Like Abraham, put your trust in him
alone. Like Enoch, walk with him and depend upon him
each day. Like Job, be patient with his timing. Like Peter,

let him change you from a reed to a rock. Like Stephen, let him plant in you a heart of forgiveness.

That is the essence of this week of readings: not that we can bid sin farewell in the weakness of the flesh. (You already have a history of failed resolutions that proves how impossible that is!) But in the power of the Holy Spirit, we can forget what is behind and press forward to maturity and to great days every day.

Say No to Bad Habits

MORNING

Have you ever struggled with a habit and finally given up? Have you ever said to yourself, "What's the use? I can't change?" Have you ever wished you could become more disciplined, a self-starter, a better budgeter of your time? Well, there's a way to handle all those handicaps.

I can say that with a fair amount of confidence, because of the progress I've experienced personally. I know what it's like to be defeated again and again by some ingrown pattern you want desperately to weed from your life. But I also know what it is to overcome some of those deficiencies and make significant progress on most of the rest.

The answer I'm suggesting is embarrassingly simple, but it works! It is this: trust God to help you conquer bad habits *one day at a time*. Notice, not overnight (though it occasionally happens that way) but one day at a time. Habits take time to form, and they take time to break.

Here's an illustration of the "secret" of such change. Once, when I was making my way through one of those mirrored mazes you find at fairs and amusement parks, I felt a tug on my jacket. I looked around and saw a little boy. He looked up at me with frightened eyes and reached out his hand. I nodded, smiled, put his little hand in mine and led him the rest of the way through the maze.

In the same way, God lets us put our hand in his. And, one step at a time, he gladly leads us out of the confusing and defeating world of stubborn patterns that block our way to becoming all we long to be.

It's nearly impossible to change old ways on our own, and even psychologists don't offer us much hope, "but with God, all things are possible . . . with him, all things become new!"

EVENING

If you are not willing to give up old ways, are you willing to be made willing? If you haven't already tried it today, decide to reach out and take the hand of Jesus tomorrow. You can't make the changes, but he can and will.

Say No to Guilt Feelings

MORNING

If you've ever thought feeling bad about something you did in the past would change things, you soon learned differently. What unresolved guilt feelings *do* change, though, is *you*. They will not change your past, but they will paralyze you in the present.

There is no greater thief of the present and future than guilt. Guilt is a good thing when it causes us to reevaluate and improve our lives. It is a good thing when it leads us to turn our lives over to God's control, receiving his forgiveness. But when it becomes an obsession, when we dwell on it so that it becomes the all-consuming thing in our lives, it destroys two of the most precious things we have—the inner peace God wants to give us, and the opportunity of making the most of today.

Are you paralyzed by guilt right now? If you are, you can find release. But it will not be enough to say to yourself, "Don't do it again," or "Others have done far worse things than I." What will help is the knowledge that God forgives sin, and a decision to act on that knowledge. There is no greater therapeutic help in the world than experiencing God's forgiveness.

Thousands of people who have experienced it have seen their whole lives changed. God has wiped out the

guilt from their pasts and, therefore, redeemed their to-
days. Because there's no longer the need to waste time
dwelling on what was, there is every opportunity to get
the most out of what's now.

EVENING

Make a list of every word or deed or omission you feel
guilty about—both from today and the past. Now, give
the list to God and ask for His forgiveness. When you
have done that, erase the list, just as you know (1 John
1:8, 9) God has forever erased them.

Say No to
a Critical Spirit

MORNING

What's your favorite pastime? Fishing? Tennis? Swimming? Table games? There's one pastime we never add to our list, even though most of us ought to.

What's the topic of conversation that begins like this: "Did you hear the latest about so and so?" Or like this: "Do you promise to keep this under your hat if I tell you?" Well, you guessed it. Right near the top of our national pastimes is the gossip game.

Now some people feel gossip is okay. A famous psychologist said, "Gossip lubricates the gears of the social engine. It's a harmless reliever of tension, an icebreaker, a remarkably effective—and painless—way to transmit substantial quantities of information. As for being malicious—sometimes it is, of course. But that's only when abused. Most gossip is simply what the dictionary says it is, 'idle talk ... about other people and their affairs.' " °

Maybe so, but the tendency to abuse gossip is great. Irrevocable harm to the reputation of the innocent is an everyday occurrence in our society. Gossip may be a reliever of tension, but it's also the author of broken marriages, ruined careers, and many a bad name. That's why the Bible makes this stern warning: "You have been

41

given freedom: not freedom to do wrong, but freedom to love and serve each other.... But if instead of showing love among yourselves you are always critical and catty, watch out! Beware of ruining each other" (Galatians 5:13, 15, *The Living Bible*).

Someone once said, "Gossip is always a personal confession, either of malice or imbecility." I would not go so far as that. Detached from a critical spirit, gossip can function positively. But let us be certain our conversation about others is that: positive; uplifting; the kind of thing we would not be afraid to say to that person face-to-face. That's how you turn this handicap into an asset.

☀

EVENING

Have you taken James' observations about the tongue seriously today? Has your conversation about others been positive or denigrating? Tomorrow, try to find something positive you can say about each person you meet.

°Joyce Brothers, quoted by David Augsburger in "Taking in Rumors?" Mennonite Hour leaflet #46. Published by *The Mennonite Hour*, Harrisonburg, Va. 22801.

Say No to a Lousy
Self-Image

MORNING

I meet a lot of people who have nothing but contempt for themselves. Nothing is more destructive. Nothing prevents us, as that does, from getting the most out of our days. As Robert Schuller has noted, "Negative tensions that rob us of peace of mind are many and far-reaching like the branches of a banyan tree. However, the taproot . . . is lack of self-esteem."

Usually a lousy self-image has its roots in the past, but whatever the causes, it severely hampers your day-to-day performance and deprives you of much of the joy of living. Here are two vital principles for handling this handicap, which I think you'll find helpful.

First, instead of dwelling on the problem you think you are, dwell, instead, on the prospect of who you could become. The friend who taught that principle to me told me that her whole life was changed when she realized that if God loved her and saw possibilities in her, she must have *some* potential worth tapping. But she also realized she would never tap it until she began to think positively about herself.

The second principle comes from the same friend. Almost at the same instant, it occurred to her that although she had little power to change the things she disliked in

43

herself, God had all power to do so. She didn't have the resources, but he did. She didn't know how to turn her weakness into strength, but God would begin doing it the moment she asked him.

"Well, did those ideas work?" I asked my friend.

"Of course!" she said. "If they hadn't, I wouldn't have told you about them!"

EVENING

Make a list of all the qualities you dislike in yourself. Now make a list of all the qualities you like in yourself. Now, compare the lists. If the first list is longer than the second, something is seriously wrong. Either you have been living your days with utter disregard for God, or you've somehow cultivated a low view of yourself. (By the way, usually the first one grows out of the second one!) If the first list is longer than the second, make a third list containing the qualities you would like to have. Now, apply the second principle from this morning's meditation. Believe it, and it shall come to pass!

Say No to Sour Grapes

MORNING

Have you ever heard the expression "sour grapes"? When you're jealous because someone else gets something you can't get, that's "sour grapes." But where did an expression like that ever come from? You'll be surprised at the answer.

The expression "sour grapes" comes from a fable told long ago by a man named Aesop. The story was about a fox in a vineyard. The fox saw a beautiful bunch of grapes that were just ripening, and he thought to himself, "Ah, that's just what I need to satisfy my thirst. A nice bunch of grapes would be even better than a soft drink," he thought. So the fox stood up on his hind feet and reached with his front paws for the grapes, but though he stretched as far as he could, he couldn't reach them.

So he backed up and ran and jumped as high as he could, but he still couldn't reach the grapes. So, finally, he decided to use his brain and got a ladder, but half way up the ladder, he lost his balance and fell down and decided to give up on the grapes.

"No big deal," he said to himself, "chances are those grapes are sour anyway; so who wants them?"

You know, it's easy to look down your nose at what you can't get. It's easy to put people down when you're

45

jealous of them, but it's also wrong. There is so much to be happy about that you can have! And there's so much to be thankful for that we all have! Isn't it sad that we have a beautiful world and a beautiful God who has given us much more than we could ever ask for, and still we remain dissatisfied.

Even when things aren't going well, if we will trust God, he always finds a way to make the best of the worst, to bring sunshine to our hearts on stormy days. So away with sour grapes, away with jealousy, away with worrying about what other people have that we don't. Instead, let's be thankful for the special blessings we do have and, thus, master the art of handling still another handicap.

EVENING

Are you becoming more sensitive to the fabulous ways God blesses you each day? List ten special blessings he has brought your way today.

Say No
to Selfishness

MORNING

The little girl in her winter coat and boots and mittens had just put her last quarter into the Salvation Army kettle. Have you ever seen a child do that? I have. Children often give with abandon—they have not learned to be cautious like us adults. They spot some Salvation Army lassie ringing her bell, and they go marching right up and gladly pitch in their last penny.

But it's not how they go up as much as how they come away that strikes me. They come away beaming every time—like they've just met God. Maybe they have! Jesus said, "To the extent that you did it to one of these brothers of mine, even the least of them, you did it to me" (Matthew 25:40, NASB).

Do you know there are a lot of people who have been playing church a good part of their lives who don't understand that Christ can be known as really, as intimately, as vitally today as he was known when he walked the paths of Galilee? They have been searching everywhere, turning over this rock and that, wishing they could have had first-hand contact with Christ, not content with the mere record of his activities in the Gospels. And they say, "If only I'd known him . . . ?" But we can know him! The moment we stop trying to possess Jesus for ourselves and

47

begin reaching out to others in love, we *will* know him! Christ becomes real through unselfish deeds.

That is a great secret that too few have realized. Many know that the way to God is through trusting him. But even those who have trusted him often haven't learned that one of the most meaningful ways to draw closer to him and to experience more of his love is through unselfishly reaching out to others in love. The way to receive love is to give love.

EVENING

Who have you met recently (today, for that matter!) with needs you can help meet? Set a plan of action tonight for doing so. Perhaps a note of encouragement is all that's required. Perhaps a thoughtful gift. Perhaps a little self-sacrifice. Whatever it is, reach out and help. That's the only way to handle the handicap of selfishness.

Say No to Deadly Routine

MORNING

A lot of people who think they're in the groove, are actually in a rut. Take my friend, Bill. Bill is the most disciplined fellow you will ever meet. But that strength is also his biggest handicap.

Bill is up at 5:00 sharp every morning. Rain or shine, he jogs five miles. He carries around little lists of details that need attending to. He is amazingly efficient and is always in control. He really seems to have it all together, and sometimes that makes me jealous.

But Bill is in trouble—with his wife, his children, and some of his friends. For although Bill seems to be in the groove, he's actually in a rut. His rigid schedule makes spontaneous family activities impossible. His two daughters feel they must have appointments to visit him at the office. His wife wonders whether she married a man or a robot.

Now, there's nothing wrong with an ordered life, but no matter how efficient our daily regimen may be, when our "fixed" agenda takes priority over relationships, something's wrong. A rut is a way of life offering no prospect of change. And every life that puts projects over people is a rut.

I am often in that rut. That is why I'm glad when Jesus

49

said, "Love your neighbor as yourself," and made it second only to loving God. He promised to give me the wherewithal to do it. The question is, am I *willing* to climb out of my rut, so I can reach out to those in need? Am I *willing* to operate flexibly enough to plunge into unplanned fun-times with my family? Am I really willing to change that much? I must be! Because the only difference between a rut and a grave is their dimensions.

EVENING

Are you a slave to routine? Do projects sometimes take precedence over people? Has that happened today? If so, outline some specific steps for eliminating it in the future.

WEEK 3

*Learn the Joy
of Loving Others*

Perspective

> *"And if you spend yourselves on behalf of the hungry and satisfy the needs of the oppressed, then your light will rise in the darkness, and your night will become like the noonday" (Isaiah 58:10).*

This passage highlights the essence of love. Love clothes the naked, feeds the hungry, shares with the poor, and assists in other concrete ways. But it is also possible to clothe the naked, feed the hungry, and help the needy without exercising love. As this text points out, real love is more than the giving of material goods, but the giving of yourself. This spending of self is the third principle for having a great day every day.

Listen to this promise in the next verse of Isaiah: "The Lord will guide you always; he will satisfy your needs in a sun-scorched land and will strengthen your frame. You will be like a well-watered garden, like a spring whose waters never fail." In other words, there is great joy in spending ourselves for others.

Of course, we don't love others just so we can receive blessing. If we are Christians, our motivation for loving others is the love we ourselves have received from God. The fact that he loved us in Christ when we were completely undeserving so overwhelms us that we are "compelled" to love others, as Paul puts it.

Nevertheless, reaching out to others in love without expecting anything in return, with no thought to the cost involved, and with a willingness to take certain risks, pays wonderful dividends. As someone put it, "Love doesn't make the world go round, but it sure does make the ride worthwhile."

Our proper motivation for loving is not to get something in return. But when we learn to show love toward each person we meet, it is nearly impossible to avoid having great days every day.

Get to Know Jesus Through Loving Others

MORNING

Wouldn't it have been great to have been with Jesus in the days of his Galilean ministry? To have walked where he walked? To have slept where he slept? To have eaten with him, talked with him, sat under his teaching, watched him perform miracles? To have personally served him?

Maybe you've never thought about that. But I often think of what it would have been like to have known some famous character of history, and of all the great men and women I know about, Jesus would have been my first choice. For one thing, I wish I could have felt his loving compassion and forgiveness firsthand. Had that been possible, there would be no doubts, no question of commitment, no struggle to find direction. Had I been able to accompany Jesus for those three years, I would be able to do what I have always wanted to do but couldn't. I would be able to shake the shackles of bad habits, poor attitudes, dull routine and uncertainty, and I'd be able to get my life put together at long last. The God question would be answered.

Do you ever think like that? Ever say to yourself, "If only I could have been there, seen him, talked with him, touched him—then, I would believe. Then, I would know beyond the shadow of a doubt that there is a God out there—a God who walked this earth of ours in the person of Jesus of Nazareth, who died to forgive us, and who rose again and is alive forevermore. Then, all my doubts would be ended, and I could really put myself into this business of being a Christian."

But haven't you seen him, talked with him, touched him? Haven't you met him? Hear the words of Jesus himself: "For I was hungry and you gave me something to eat, I was thirsty and you gave me something to drink, I was a stranger and you invited me in, I needed clothes and you clothed me, I was sick and you looked after me, I was in prison and you came to visit me" (Matthew 25:35, 36).

✷

EVENING

Have you learned to see Jesus in the eyes of those who need your love? What opportunities for loving and serving others did you have today? How well did you do?

Learn the Art of Risky Loving

MORNING

Does anybody care anymore? The other day someone told me about a television program—one of those hidden camera programs. A little boy was planted on a city street. Whenever someone passed by, he told them he was lost and asked for help in making a phone call. But almost no one took the time to help.

"I'm too busy," they would say. "Sorry, kid." "Why don't you go ask that policeman down there?" Person after person walked by and refused to help the little boy. Either they didn't have time, or they just didn't feel like getting involved.

Back in 1928, a young man was lying on a boat dock soaking up some sun. All at once he saw a man fall out of a boat, and it was obvious the man could not swim. The man on the boat dock was a strong swimmer; nevertheless, he was resting at the moment, so he simply watched the struggling man until he disappeared beneath the water forever.

Afterwards there was a lawsuit. But the court found the man on the dock had no responsibility to try to save the other man's life. It was his option to respond or not respond.

The cost of malpractice insurance has multiplied astonishingly. And the fear of such a suit keeps many physicians from offering help to persons who desperately need it. In some emergency situations, doctors are actually afraid to help the persons they've dedicated their lives to helping.

So, even the laws of the land make it difficult to reach out and be a friend in our day! But which is more important—minding our own business, keeping to ourselves, not getting involved, or the recognition that we live in a world that requires dependence on each other? I think it's the latter. In the words of John Donne, "No man is an island." Or in the words of the Apostle Paul, "No man lives unto himself, and no man dies unto himself." So, maybe we don't have to answer to the local magistrate, but one day we'll have to answer to a higher one.

EVENING

What expressions of caring have you shown today? Name three persons whose needs you could help.

Let Your Loving Start at Home

MORNING

Like the little boy or little girl who'd rather do the neighbor's work than Dad's or Mom's, we often overlook those who are closest to us. We seek to help our neighbors; we reach out to needy people overseas; but we forget about the needy people right in our own home.

Every once in awhile I discover that one of the persons closest to me has been crying out, "Please help me," and I haven't noticed. I keep so busy writing and speaking and teaching and pastoring a church, I tend to forget my best energies need to be applied right at home.

For if I speak with the eloquence of a Shakespearean actor, possess the gift of a prolific pen, and have faith enough to attempt a thousand impossible tasks at once, but have no love, I am like a candidate without votes or a computer without a brain.

Have you been learning that lesson, too? Have you been learning to love your child more? And have you been learning to love your wife more? While most husbands get their self-esteem from their work, many wives get their self-esteem from their relationship with their husband. Yet, I read just recently somewhere that the average husband spends less than 15 minutes per week talking about relational matters with his wife.

Or, if you're a wife, are you learning to love your husband more? A few years ago a cookbook came out which had a section on preserving husbands. It pointed out that some wives like to keep their husbands in a pickle, while others prefer to keep them in hot water. It further pointed out that even poor varieties of husbands can be made tender and good with a garnish of patience, the flavoring of a kiss, and the sweetening of a smile. Prepare your husband like that, the cookbook said, and he'll keep for years.

So, wife, husband, son, or daughter, why not ask God today—right now—to help you love your family more? That's where our love needs to begin.

EVENING

What can you do to demonstrate your love for your family members or close friends? Think of some little kindnesses you could follow through with tomorrow. And, by the way, how did you do today?

Love God Through Loving Others

MORNING

Tommy had never been interested in God until he learned he had terminal cancer. Then, he began beating frantically on the doors of heaven, only there was no answer. So, he quit. He decided there must be something better he could do with the rest of his life than calling out to someone who wasn't there.

Then some words floated into Tommy's mind—something his teacher, John Powell, had said: "The essential sadness is to go through life without loving. But it would be almost equally sad to go through life and leave this world without ever telling those you loved that you had loved them."°

So (starting with the hardest), he told his Dad, "I love you." His Dad cried and hugged him. Then he said to his mother and little brother, "I love you," and they cried and hugged him, too. Then the most remarkable thing happened. One day Tommy turned around and God was there. God didn't come when Tommy wanted him just for himself. But when Tommy reached out in love, God was suddenly there!

I feel quite sure that is the sort of thing Henry Ward Beecher had in mind when he told his congregation, "Love is that regent quality which was meant to reveal the divine to us. It carries its own light and, by its own secret nature, is drawn instantly toward God, and reflects the knowledge of him back upon us." And it seems likely that's what the Apostle Paul had in mind when he wrote, "But now abide faith, hope, love, these three; but the greatest of these is love."

So, what I am suggesting today is this. If you're looking to get closer to God, to experience more of his love, perhaps one way to begin is to reach out in love to others. Nothing helps to make your faith come alive like experiencing God's love in that way.

EVENING

Does loving others come first in your life? Let your acts and words from today answer the question.

°John Powell, *Unconditional Love* (Niles, Ill.: Argus Communications, 1978), pp. 113-114.

Love out of Gratitude

MORNING

I live in New England, but I often have a chance to fly somewhere like New York, Ontario, or Oregon. However, whether I'm in the Blue Ridge Mountains of Virginia or on the streets of Pasadena, one thing remains constant—the people. People are the same everywhere and in every generation. And you know, that's what I love most about every place I go—the people I meet.

Would you like to know why I love people so? It's because God loves them. If God thought people were worth loving, then so do I.

I've discovered from experience that people *are* worth loving, too, because no matter how tarnished their lives are, due to sin, no matter how confused they are, no matter how deeply hurt, when I let the love of God shine through I've noticed that something inside of them begins to change. Little by little even those who seemed most unlovable at first attract more and more of my affection.

But I have an even stronger motivation to love people—gratitude. Helen Keller said, "There is no lovelier way to thank God for your sight than by giving a helping hand to someone in the dark." When I remember that Helen Keller was blind and deaf, that really strikes home. I was blind and deaf once, too, in the spiritual sense. So do I dare go my own way and forget those who are still there—who are still without God? No way! Real gratitude means *more* than giving thanks, it means reaching out in love to others.

EVENING

Is your gratitude articulate? Do you say thanks to God through loving others? How did you speak your gratitude today?

Love If You Would Receive Love

MORNING

Did you ever pray to God in some crisis and have the feeling you were praying to an empty universe? That's the most forsaken feeling in the world, isn't it? I've discovered that there's a better way to get in touch with God at such times.

We all need love. That's just the way God made us. We need the love of God, and we need the love of others. But usually the way we go about getting that love is by going around looking for it. However, on those occasions when God chooses to remain very distant, he reminds us that that's precisely how *not* to love. Just as we have friends by being a friend, so we find love by giving it. And when we find love by giving love, we find God. That's the way it always works. God touches us when we touch others. As one writer put it:

> *I sought my soul*
> *But my soul I could not see.*
> *I sought my God,*
> *But my God eluded me.*
> *I sought my brother,*
> *And I found all three.*
> *—Anonymous*

When will we learn at last that people are for loving and things are for using, not vice versa? When will we learn that the way to reach out to God is to reach out to others? And when will we learn that it is only as we reach out in love to others, we are enabled to find and feel the love of God? As we noticed in Monday's reading, Jesus put it this way: "Whatever you do for one of the least of my brothers, you do to me." So, next time you call out to God and there's no answer, remember that, and reach out to someone in need with the same love you yourself are seeking.

EVENING

Next time you feel discouraged, here are ten things you can do to help yourself: First, go out and do something for someone else—then, repeat it nine times. Maybe you thought of a way to help someone today. Did you follow through? Then, you know what I mean when I say the surest way to get close to God is by reaching out to others.

Learn the Joy of Loving Others

MORNING

In one of Tolstoy's stories, an old cobbler named Martin is reading his Bible, wondering what it would have been like to have had a visit from Jesus. He dozes off and is startled by a voice saying, "Martin, look into the street tomorrow. I will come."

Martin isn't sure whether the voice is real or his imagination. It certainly seemed real. But that is too much to hope for, he thinks. Nevertheless, Martin is at his window constantly during the next day. As the day progresses (a blustery, snowy day), Martin invites a street sweeper into his little room. He offers him tea and a chance to warm his hands over the stove. Then he invites in a soldier's wife whom he sees from the window trying to keep her baby warm. Then Martin invites an apple woman in, along with a lad who has just stolen one of her apples. Martin helps her quell her anger, and she leaves with the boy helping her with her load. The cobbler sees other people through his window, too, but no Jesus.

The old man has about given up hope when once again the voice calls out to him, "Martin, don't you recognize me?" It is the snow sweeper. Then the voice speaks again, and it is the soldier's wife. Then the voice speaks once more, and it is the apple woman.

Suddenly Martin realized the truth we've been considering this week: "Whatever you do for one of the least of my brothers, you do to me," said Jesus. In reaching out in love to others, the old cobbler has reached out and drawn near to Christ himself.

☀

Reread Matthew 25:31-40. Has it come alive for you this week? How can you make it an even greater reality in your life?

WEEK 4

*Cultivate Your
Friendships*

Perspective

*"The entire law is summed up in a single command:
'Love your neighbor as yourself'" (Galatians 5:14).*

Everyone needs friends. When a crisis comes along, when family relationships begin to fall apart, when self-esteem is low, or when we just feel lonely, friends come in and fill the gap, boost our morale, affirm our strengths, and offer helpful counsel.

But this week we are not so much concerned with what your friends can mean to you as with what you can mean to them. The first and greatest mistake we can make in a friendship is to think of it in terms of what we get out of it. Every deep friendship brings wonderful benefits. The returns, in fact, sometimes overwhelm us, especially when things are tough. But it is wise always to think of those blessings as happy by-products of a friendship and not as the goal.

In the first place, giving your friendship to others is a rewarding experience in itself. To be attentive, available, and affirming to your friends is the sort of activity that gives your day meaning and value. You feel you are doing something worthwhile, and that alone can turn a bland day into a great one. Likewise, watching the power of your friendship turn a frown into a smile, desperation to hope, retreat into advance, or frustration to relief, is an exhilarating experience.

71

So cultivate your friendships, but recognize that the benefits that come from them must neither be the cause nor the basis for relationships. To be sure, friendship does work two ways, but it is not a 50-50 proposition. Ideal friendship is 100 percent given both ways.

Give Your Friends Room

MORNING

Have you ever thought over the relationships in your past that somehow didn't make it? Think especially of those relationships you decided to drop or not pursue. What did they have in common? What was it that turned you off? Chances are I can tell you on my first guess.

When we examine our aborted former relationships, we discover that usually we backed off for one of only a handful of reasons. One reason especially stands out. Nobody likes to be dominated. We all need friendships, but we also need freedom. So when we review our past, we find that we've tended to back off from those relationships in which we felt manipulated or boxed in. Because of their need to dominate, control, judge, those friends scarcely gave us room to breathe. So rather than suffocate, we abandoned the relationship.

Well, if that's the way we've responded in certain situations, we can be quite sure our friends feel the same way. So we need to be very careful about our own tendency to manipulate, too. In friendships we need to give each other space. We are entitled to our own opinions and our own tastes. We are entitled to be ourselves. Furthermore, we're entitled to our own private feelings and thoughts, and friends who try to invade the inner space of one another automatically undermine the relationship.

73

Just as Jesus came to earth to free us to be all we can be, so we need to give growing room to our friends. We need to remember *we* don't change people. God changes people. We need to challenge one another, we need to be role models for one another, we need to encourage one another, and we need to build each other up, but at the same time give our friends space.

EVENING

Have you been domineering in any of your relationships today? If so, how could you have handled yourself more acceptably? If not, what steps might you take to help a friend who tends to be dominating?

Be Attentive

MORNING

Here's a question I feel quite sure you can identify with. When people are speaking to you, do you ever find your mind racing ahead to your response even before they are done talking? Do you plan your answer before they've finished getting out what they have to say? Well, there is a reason for that.

The average rate of speech is about 125 words a minute. But the average person thinks four times faster than that. That's why people on the listening side of a conversation often get carried away by their own thoughts. It's not really that your mind wanders, or that your attention span is short, but rather, you anticipate what is going to be said and jump ahead of where your friend actually is in his conversation.

But although that's the way things are, that's not the way they should be. We need to recognize that hearing and listening are two different things. And even though it's difficult, and requires diligent effort, we need to work hard at really hearing our friends out. Otherwise, we will merely be talking past each other. Otherwise, there will be constant miscommunication. Otherwise, our relationships will be undercut rather than enhanced.

Few of us recognize the importance of sensitivity in a relationship. That wasn't true of Jesus, however. Again and again the New Testament reveals that Jesus was a careful listener and careful observer. He was sensitive to people's needs. He was sensitive to their heartaches. In all of his encounters he showed that he really cared, and he also showed that he understood.

A relationship is only as good as its communication. Communication is the most important factor in bringing two people together. Whether it's our coming together with Jesus, a friend, or a family member, therefore, careful attentive listening is a must.

EVENING

Think about the conversations you had today. Who did most of the talking? How attentive were you? Honestly now, did you make a solid effort to hear the messages behind the words, or did you hear only the words themselves?

Be Available

"Ken, more than anything else, what do you appreciate about your wife?" I asked. Because he'd been my friend for many years, I knew there were many things about Peg he liked, but I was interested in what stood out above all the other things. "What do I appreciate most about her?" he repeated. "Why, that's easy!" he said suddenly, snapping his fingers.

Ken then explained that the thing he appreciated most about his wife was her availability to him. "When I have a problem, when I am down, when I am wrestling with a tough decision, Peggy's always there," he said. "I can count on her."

I've thought a lot about it, and I'm convinced my friend's focus of appreciation is not misplaced. Whether you are talking about bosom buddies or partners in a marriage relationship, friends need to be *together*. They need to be available to one another. No friendship, no growing relationship can be without it. Even though busy friends may have to go out of their way to make a meeting possible, it is always well worthwhile to do so. Being together is essential to becoming close, and the most satisfying way of being together is physical presence.

That's how God sought to show his friendship toward man. Through the person of Jesus, he sought to make

77

himself available. And the life of Jesus models the meaning of that availability. Jesus was always where he could be found. He was always identifying himself with people. He did not lead a sheltered life. He visited large cities and small villages. He taught in the marketplaces and on the street corners. He accepted opportunities for ministry as they occurred: he kept no office hours; he was willing to help someone in need anytime, anywhere; his pulpit and his counseling room always went with him. And he's available today, too, for those who seek him. He's available to you. He wants to be your friend, too.

EVENING

How available are you to potential friends and established friends? Did you put anybody off today? Did you postpone any appointments today? Think of one of your closest friends: does he/she know you are available when there is a need? How?

Be Affirming

MORNING

I have a friend who goes out of his way to find something positive and affirming to say whenever we meet. If you think that kind of supportive attitude in a friend doesn't enhance and build up the relationship—well, you should see what it's done for us. I guarantee you'd be convinced.

I suppose it's possible for praise to be carried too far. Samuel Johnson said, "He who praises everybody, praises nobody." But I would rather err on the side of being too free with my praise, than on the side of withholding it altogether, for praise—affirmation—is one of the surest ingredients for building a friendship. Mark Twain said, "I can live for two months on a good compliment." He was speaking for us all.

One of the reasons we tend to withhold affirmation is the individualistic mood of contemporary society. Everyone is out for himself. Everyone is looking out for number one. So when our friends succeed, we tend to be a bit jealous, and sometimes we even try to put down the success of our friends. But wherever that is happening, you can be sure the relationship is on shaky ground.

In the church of Jesus Christ there is no room for such an attitude. The Bible describes Jesus' church as a body, and it says that each person in the church is like some part

79

of the body. Some are hands, some are eyes, some are lips, and so on, and all the parts are dependent upon each other. Even the seemingly most insignificant parts are vital. So Christians delight in each other's talents and applaud each other's successes. It is part of a totally new attitude they receive when they become Christians by inviting Jesus to take control of their lives.

New attitudes can awaken in you, too. But you don't create them, Jesus Christ does.

EVENING
Name five instances in which you affirmed others today. Name five more ways in which you could have affirmed others.

Be Honest

MORNING

Sometimes it is difficult to be honest with your friend. You're afraid of hurting his feelings, afraid he won't understand, afraid he'll become defensive, afraid your friendship will disintegrate on the spot. So, instead of clearing the air, instead of getting things out in the open, you clam up.

We talk a lot about honesty. We say that honesty is the best policy. We say we need to be able to trust each other. We say we need to be candid with our friends. But even though most of us would like our friends to be honest with us, even though we'd like to know when something is wrong, somehow we imagine that our friends will simply not tolerate similar candor from us. So we beat around the bush, we avoid open, truthful communication like the plague without realizing that all the while our subtle dishonesty is nibbling away at the integrity of our friendship.

Robert Louis Stevenson said, "We are all travelers in this world, and the best companion we can find in our travels is an honest friend." Stevenson was right. Deception and friendship simply cannot live side by side. Take away honesty and you take away the very foundation of friendship. That doesn't mean honesty involves telling everything, but it does mean a sharing of concerns, expectations, and disappointments in the relationship. It does involve clearing the air when a cloud has come over the relationship. It does involve the kind of truthfulness that's necessary to help each other grow. The Bible says Jesus always demonstrated that kind of candor in his relationships. It grew, not so much out of a passion for the truth, as a passion for his friends. In the same manner he expects us to love our friends so that we're not afraid of the truth—of giving or receiving it. True friendship is strengthened by candid, clear communication; and it is welcomed.

EVENING

Did you shy away from being candid with someone today? When you do shy away from candor, why do you do so?

Learn the Importance of Trust

MORNING

Billy had been betrayed once too often. Time after time she had believed the good intentions of so-called friends, and they had abused her trust. So she wasn't about to trust me. Billy was in trouble, and I could help her. But her mistrust might spoil all I wanted to do.

Recently I was visiting a youth camp, and I was shown what they called a ropes course. It was really a kind of obstacle course, but it was designed to teach some important lessons. One of those lessons is trust. Some of the obstacles are impossible to accomplish without putting total trust in your buddies. In the same way, I couldn't help Billy unless she was willing to trust me. (Fortunately, she did.) And in the same way, it's impossible to build friendships without trust. We need to trust that our friend is going to keep our secret. And *we* must learn how to keep confidence, too. When *we* share confidences, we expect our friends to be discreet and not reveal publicly what they've heard from us in private, and in the same way, our friends need to be able to expect that from us.

I told you how my friend Billy had difficulty in trusting me because of the betrayal of others. In the film *The Lady Sings the Blues*, another Billy—Billy Holliday, a jazz vocalist of the 1930s and 1940s—was unable to trust people for the same reason. Her trust had been so abused by people she thought were her friends, that finally she turned to dope. More and more her affection turned to her dogs. In the end her pets were really her only trusted friends.

Jesus is our model of trusting. For example, just think of how he's trusted us to do the right thing with our lives, giving us the freedom to choose his way or reject it. That's the way we need to trust our friends. "Trust men, and they will be true to you," said Emerson. "Treat them greatly, and they will show themselves great."

EVENING

Ralph Waldo Emerson said, "Trust men, and they will be true to you." Do your friends trust you? Why do they trust you or not trust you?

Don't Forget the Little Things

MORNING

From his friend, a journalist received a 15-cent plastic pencil sharpener. A wife receives a single rose from her husband—just on impulse—a spontaneous token of his love. We have no idea what an impact little things have on the growth of a friendship.

When it comes to friendships, little things are big things. Just as letters add up to words, words add up to sentences, sentences add up to paragraphs, and so on, so little thoughtful gestures even gestures as simple as a compliment, a stroke, or an inexpensive gift—amount to more than we can possibly measure in the building of a relationship. Dave Wilkerson said, "Love is not something you say; love is something you do." I like that, but it doesn't suggest the spectacular, it suggests the accumulation of little deeds of kindness, which build up the relationship, as someone put it, "like a fine lacquer finish is built up with many layers, one upon the other."

Interestingly, that's often one of the first ways you know a friendship is going sour—when those little acts of kindness cease. But although the small things we do for a friend may seem simple, they really require effort. It's easy to let the opportunity to express care pass. It's easy to wait till the next birthday, or the next anniversary. But for those little acts of kindness and care to become a part of our lifestyle, we need to put forth imaginative and creative effort. That little gift needs to fit the person. That kind word may necessarily be the result of careful listening. So a kind heart may indeed be a fountain of gladness, but it's never automatic. Kindness is "a language the dumb can speak and the deaf can hear and understand," but it is a language only the heart of compassion can produce.

EVENING

What little things have you done for friends today? Have you made any phone calls, written any notes, given any encouragement, or given any surprises? How have little things had an impact on your friendship with others?

WEEK 5

Get Your Priorities in Order

Perspective

*"But seek first his kingdom and his righteousness,
and all these things will be given to you as well" (Matthew 6:33).*

One of the most important principles on the way to
having a great day every day is to get your priorities in
order. A better life is possible for all of us if we make that
a top goal.

Each of us has the opportunity to choose the kind of
life we want to live and to decide what we want to accomplish. Sometimes, of course, unexpected barriers crop up.
Sometimes closed doors, illness, and other factors beyond
our control get in the way. But the desire to put our
priorities in order is one goal almost no obstacle can get in
the way of—if we are relying on God for our strength.

We may have setbacks. We may fail and have to try
again. But if we know where we are going and our aim is
to stay on course whatever the cost, we will not be turned
back from our goal. We will give priority to such pursuits
as serving God first of all, living a more modest lifestyle,
being more compassionate toward others, growing in
character and integrity and morality, or any other priority
that reflects God's will rather than purely selfish pursuits.

One thing more is important to consider as we begin
our week of considering some new priorities. We talk
about goals but in a sense the goal of getting our priorities
in order is a lifelong task. We never completely achieve it.

But we must always remember: not achieving all our goals is no disaster, but not having goals is.

Take a New Look at What Comes First

MORNING

What we believe ultimately shapes our lives. If we believe in quiet, we choose to live where we can have a quiet existence. If we believe in the importance of the extended family, we make plans to be near our family. Many believe in money. They believe in its power to make dreams come true. And there's no question about it—money *is* powerful, money *does* make dreams come true. But *what* dreams?

Suppose I asked that of you. What are your dreams? What, in the end, do you want for your life? Who would you like to become? Do you want to remain the person you are now? The dreams you build your life around shape who you become.

We live in the most affluent society in the history of man. But our dreamers have grown few; our visions end with ourselves. We are affluent, but spiritually impoverished. We have so focused our lives around prosperity that we have forgotten what it is to dream, forgotten that the true measure of a life is its quality, forgotten that true prosperity is the presence of joy, peace, and love, and that anything else is to settle for second best.

Jesus said, "Where your treasure is, there will your heart be also." What you value most is what you become.

The decisions you make today determine the kind of person you will be in ten years. Who do you want to become? What is your treasure?

EVENING

What priorities are you building your life around? Is there any evidence of it in how you conducted your affairs today? What do you think your priorities say about your beliefs?

Take a New Look
at Your Lifestyle

MORNING

Someone said of Ernest Hemingway's stripped-down style of writing, "Its beauty lies in its simplicity." You can also say that about the Christian life. In a day of complexity, there's a way of life that makes our difficult choices manageable and helps bring our loose ends together.

"How I wish I could simplify my life," my friend, Helen, said to me. "You can," I immediately replied. Then I said to myself, "Art McPhee, who are you to say that?" For I lead a very full life of pastoring, traveling, teaching, writing, and recording for radio. But, then I thought, "Well, yes, all that's true; nevertheless, even with all I have to do, I still lead a fairly relaxed life."

So, I went on: "Helen, I believe simple, uncomplicated living is accomplished much differently than most people imagine. For example, can you think of anyone whose life was more straightforward and simple than Jesus' was? Yet, his life was as full of work and activity as anyone's who's ever lived.

"Jesus' days were filled with teaching, healing, advice, reaching out to the unloved, traveling from place to place—with all sorts of grueling activity. Yet, you can honestly say of him that he led a simple life. He had time

93

for prayer, time for meditation, time for his friends, time for simple pleasures with common folk and uncommon folk, too. He was never rushed, never tense, never mentally exhausted, and he was never demoralized by not getting things done.

"Helen," I said, "I believe if we would model our lives after Jesus, we would be able to move from complexity to simplicity, too."

EVENING

Compare your attitude toward all the things you had to do today with the attitude of Jesus. Jesus had even more packed into his days than you, yet he still had time for prayer and the simple joys of life. How can you find more time for such things in your day? Do you consider your present priorities a help or a hindrance in doing so?

Take a New Look at People

MORNING

I have a recurring thought at funerals. When I look at all those flowers, and see all those tears, and hear the fine compliments that are given to the one who's passed on, I wonder if they ever got flowers or compliments when they were alive, or I wonder if anyone ever wept with them when they were sad.

We live in an impersonal world. We don't take time for people anymore. In fact, some people are more involved with the characters in their favorite TV soap opera than they are with the people they live and work with. So people get hurt, and we don't care. Even in our homes, urgent needs are sometimes greeted with apathy and unconcern. And the deep inner needs of the persons closest to us go undetected. The well-known political novel, *Advice and Consent,* has coined a metaphor for our day, "The age of the shrug." There's a lot of truth in that. And because of it, we miss a lot of joy.

It's not that we intend to neglect our loved ones. Sometimes we are merely playing the going-to-do-it-later game. If you miss sending your wife flowers for Christmas, "Well, there's always Easter," you reason. If you miss complimenting your husband on his job promotion, "Well, he's due for another promotion next year."

But whenever we play the "later" game, not only do we risk robbing others of the compassion, comfort, or congratulations they deserve, we fail to live up to God's expectation of us—the expectation that above all else in this world, we are to love each other. In the long run, loving our neighbors is second to loving God. But we need to start doing it right now; when those we love are gone, it will be too late. "By this all men will know you are my disciples," Jesus said, "that you love one another."

EVENING

You observed in your reading of John 11 this morning how deeply Jesus cared for people. As you retrace your steps today, what evidence is there of your concern for people? How could you have demonstrated you care about people even better than you did?

Take a New Look at Character

MORNING

I have come to love hiking, as much for the fragrance of woodland flowers and herbs and shrubs, as for any other reason. The creatures of the fields and forests have their own special perfumes, too. Take butterflies, for instance. Ever hear of a chocolate butterfly?

Male butterflies often release distinctive scents from special glands. Their flavors have been variously described as honeysuckle, sandlewood, sweet pea, heliotrope, and even chocolate—depending on the brand and the reporter, I guess.

There's another kind of fragrance that *people* exude. You might call it character aroma. It's a feel you get when you're with them. It has to do with how they affect others—sometimes like a perfume, sometimes like a poison.

I'm convinced that is true of all of us. We all have some kind of distinctive scent. And we can't hide it. There's no touching, hearing or seeing it, but it's there just the same, and others are always conscious of it.

I'm thinking of more than reputation though. I'm thinking of character. Character is like a flower and reputation like its fragrance. The fragrance is what people think of it; the flower is the real thing.

I am always falling short of my goal of a Christlike character. But there's a verse in the Bible that prods me to keep on working at loving others as Jesus did—with a selfless love that does not depend upon reciprocity. Here's the way the verse goes: "Thanks be to God who ... through us spreads everywhere the fragrance of the knowledge of him" (2 Corinthians 2:15). That means that God can perfume this foul and bitter world of ours with the love of Christ through you and me! And who, in the whole universe, is better able to perfume the world with love and peace than him?

EVENING

Did the fragrance of the love of Christ linger where you walked today? How are you doing in appropriating the new character Christ wants to give you? Which fruits of the Spirit need to come out more in your life?

Take a New Look at Integrity

MORNING

Could Walter Cronkite *really* be elected president of the United States? We laugh, for he has never expressed any interest in elected office. Nevertheless, for many, Cronkite epitomizes that quality we seem to value most in a person—integrity; a man of conviction.

It's been my experience that people admired most are not held in high esteem for their beauty, their intelligence, or their wealth. While people with those qualities attract attention and are in the spotlight, respect isn't always what we feel. Cronkite isn't trusted because he's a pretty face; he's trusted because he communicates moral integrity.

But moral integrity is becoming a rarity. The evidence indicates we live in a time of moral decay. For example, pornography is now a $4 billion a year business—exceeding the movie and music business industry combined. The typical customer is a white, middle-class businessman. Not an unshaved, greasy-haired, trench-coated man in black, but a family man in a coat and tie.

Rivaling pornography as a sign of our times is abortion on demand. In the United States one unborn baby is killed by abortion every 30 seconds. The number of abortions since 1973 now exceeds the total number of Jews killed in the concentration camps by the Nazis during Hitler's regime.

Where have our convictions gone? How has our moral compass become so broken? Tell me, do you live according to your convictions? A friend once asked me: "If you were on trial for being a Christian, would there be enough evidence to convict you?"

The apostle Paul wrote: "I am not ashamed of the gospel of Jesus Christ." It should be our deeply held hope that we may never live as ones ashamed of the gospel of Jesus Christ, but as those fully willing to live out our convictions in every sphere of life.

EVENING

Did your conduct today bear witness to the strength of your convictions? Set a goal for tomorrow (and every day) to carry out your tasks and make your decisions without compromise. Make a list of specific ways God can assist you to accomplish your goal; then ask him for the help you need.

Take a New Look at Morality

MORNING

Old Andrew Jackson, great thinker that he was, said one time that "it is a mighty poor mind that cannot think of more than one way to spell a word." (I am glad my secretary didn't say that!) It is, of course, true that certain choices can be left to our personal whims, but not all of them. Certainly not in the moral realm, for example.

There used to be a time when you could know what was expected of you, and when words like "truth" and "purity" had real meaning. Today the only people who use such words seem to be the folks at the Food and Drug Administration.

The world today, it seems to me, suffers not only from a lack of rugged convictions, but also from timidity in expressing the convictions it has. Far too many of us are suffering from moral laryngitis.

Lately I've been wondering why, and one of the possible reasons that popped into my mind is that perhaps we've been hoodwinked into believing that Andy Jackson's freewheeling approach to spelling can somehow have as one of its many counterparts, a freewheeling approach to morality.

Is that the reason we don't speak out? Have we decided that morality is merely a matter of personal preferences? Maybe, but that is hard for me to believe, for we have seen the consequences of that kind of thinking in more broken homes and hearts than ever before. We have seen the consequences in the skyrocketing crime rate. For example, there have been more killings by gunshot wounds in this country since 1900 than there have been in all the wars we've fought.

The power to speak out is ours if we will only take it. We gain nothing by ignoring or kidding ourselves about where we are headed if we allow our moral convictions to continue to deteriorate. But our speaking out doesn't need to be all negative, because the good news of Jesus' resurrection tells us that God is still in control of this world, and he offers to all who will receive it the strength and guidance to follow a new way—the way of righteousness.

EVENING

Have you stood for what is right today? Both in your speech and your actions? Why must speaking and living your convictions always go together? How do they complement each other?

Take a New Look at Peer Pressure

MORNING

Halford Luccock was convinced that if you scoop out the brain of any chance person coming down the street and exchange it with someone else's brain, the difference probably won't be detected for several months.

It's tragic how few authentic individuals are left in the world. Most of us are just carbon copies, one of a particular herd. It may be the conservative herd, the liberal herd, the God-and-country herd, or the buy-the-latest-fashions herd. But what we fail to realize is that whenever we allow a group to do our thinking for us and bow in obeisance to the idol of conformity, we give consent to the tragedy of the sort of carbon-copy generation that becomes the puppet of the first tyrant who happens along.

I don't know about you, but I get scared to death when I see news reels of some army of robots goose-stepping by with no one out of step. "Those are not people," I think, "they are machines!" The individual members are, at best, one-dimensional paper doll people.

The herd mentality has resulted in some of the greatest atrocities of history. Jesus was crucified, because Pilate was afraid of an early morning mob. Millions of Jews were slaughtered in the holocaust of World War II, because Hitler was able to drown out the voice of the individual.

The Bible has a word to the wise to say about all this. It's simple, but profound: "Don't let the world squeeze you into its mold." Instead, let Jesus Christ transform and free your mind.

EVENING

Which do you worry about most: what Christ thinks or what your peers think? Can you think of anything you did today because of peer pressure and against your better judgement? How could you have dealt better with the situation?

Overcome the Tyranny of the Urgent

Perspective

*"Teach us to number our days aright, that we may
gain a heart of wisdom" (Psalm 90:12).*

When Moses prayed these words, asking God to help
us number our days, he wasn't simply asking for a sense
of how much of life was left. Rather, he was asking for an
ongoing sense of the importance of each day and the
need to fill it with worthwhile, God-honoring activity.

We number our days not by counting how many are
left, but by our daily prayers, our daily obedience, our
daily acts of love, our daily sense of our responsibility as
stewards of the time God has given us.

Most people these days are time conscious. In fact,
some people are so obsessed by the hours and minutes of
a day that they are actually bound by them. As we think
about overcoming the tyranny of the urgent this week,
that sort of thinking—packing every minute full—is not
what we have in mind at all. We want to accomplish what
we can. We want to find ways to use our time more
wisely. We want to be better organized. But our main
concern is to be the masters of our time, not allowing time
to be the master of us.

The best way to achieve this is to recognize why God
has put us here. There's nothing sadder than people who
do not know why they were born into this world until
they are ready to go out of it. Almost as sad is the plight of
Christians who are saved *from* sin, but who take years to

discover that they are saved *for* something: loving acts of witness and service as God's ambassadors.

So we're not talking about counting days as we would count our money. We are not simply interested in how much time is left, nor are we merely interested in crowding as much as we can into each hour. Those concerns are valid to a point, but our primary concern is to invest quality time for God, and to emerge from each day knowing that we have turned what could have been a day full of trivial pursuits into a great day of significant ones.

Remember, Your Time Is Not Your Own

MORNING

Whenever a new year comes around, I look forward to receiving a number of new calendars. One I hang on the wall next to my desk. Another I put on the desk itself. And still another I carry in my wallet. I possess a couple more calendars too, but, sometimes they possess me.

If you've never experienced the tyranny of a full calendar, you're more fortunate than I. I'm one of those persons who has a hard time saying no, and no sooner do I receive a new calendar than it begins to get filled with meetings and engagements.

What does it say about us when we make more appointments than we can keep and set more deadlines than we can meet? What does it say when, instead of being opportunities, the days on our calendars become a source of worry and stress? When I ask those questions, my mind goes back to Jesus, who accomplished more in his short lifetime than anyone who's ever lived. Yet, there was a relaxed pace about his life that is the envy of us all. He knew how to edit his appointment book masterfully. How did he do it?

First, he started each day with God. Early in the morning he would go off to some solitary spot and receive his marching orders. Once his disciples burst right into his quiet time with God and demanded, "Where have you been? Everybody's looking for you." Jesus' reply was, "Maybe so, but we can't stay. God's orders for today are to move on."

You see, Jesus was keenly aware that time is not our own; we are merely the trustees of it. Time is to be used for God's purposes, not our own. Furthermore, Jesus had clear priorities. He knew what his purpose was. And every moment was dedicated to that end.

Why not put these principles to work yourself and let today be a wonderful turning point in your life? You'll get more time out of your life, not to mention more life out of your time!

EVENING

Was your day too full today? Read again Mark 1:35-39. What vital lessons can you learn about planning your day from this passage?

Make a "To Do" List

MORNING

"How do you live on 24 hours a day?" Ever ask yourself that? I have. Often! And friends who know something about my schedule ask it of me, too.

The truth is that 24-hour days have been all *anybody's* ever had. Yet, there are men and women who have used their time magnificently better than the rest of us. Think of the accomplishments of a man like Leonardo da Vinci, for example. Accomplished artist, inventor, anatomist, sculptor, architect, and engineer, his breadth of creativity and his list of successes boggles the minds of most of us. But there are also people we know personally who have long records of outstanding accomplishments, too. They may not have da Vinci's creative genius, but they do have his genius for getting the most out of every moment.

How do they do it? How can you do it? One key way is through a simple device called a "To Do List." Ask a friend, who has lots to do and consistently gets it done, how he does it, and he will probably mention that he makes a daily list of things to be accomplished.

Try it yourself. Write down long-range goals as well as immediate ones. Then prioritize them, and one at a time get each task out of the way. Include things other than professional tasks, though. Include time for God, for your family, for other people, and for yourself. Whenever you

111

can, delegate—especially if others can do the job more efficiently or effectively than you.

The Bible teaches us to make the most of our time. Sometimes the key is not to work harder, but smarter.

EVENING

Did you work according to a plan today? Do you regularly make out a "To Do List"? Do you regularly set goals? Make a list of your accomplishments today; how would you evaluate your performance? Did you work harder, or smarter, than yesterday?

Make the Most of Each Day's Opportunities

MORNING

Three things never return: the spoken word, yesterday, and the wasted opportunity. Let me ask you about the last one: are you satisfied with how you use your opportunities?

What is life other than a series of opportunities that you can either redeem or throw away? I need not convince you of that—you know it as well as I do. But most of us have to admit we've thrown away too many opportunities anyway. Why do we do it when we know better?

I can only guess that your reasons are some of mine. First, I have not reminded myself as often as I need to that time is a gift from God, a gift more valuable than gold. Second, I have not fostered my inner conviction that I am a steward of my time, and accountable for how I use it. Third, I've not gotten into the habit of balancing my time judgments with my value judgments. And, finally, I have not worked hard enough to establish good work habits.

For example, think of all the little time wasters we allow to intrude upon our time, like watching television or failing to have clear goals and priorities. All are opportunity killers.

How can you develop the will to fight these known

113

enemies? Here are some suggestions. First, acknowledge your responsibility as a steward of each day's 24 hours. Second, set clear goals that are in line with God's will for your life. Third, employ the age-old tactic of "divide and conquer." Begin with the easy time wasters. Identify them and win over them one at at ime. Then, gradually move on to the more difficult ones, always reminding yourself that when you've gotten hold of your opportunities, you've gotten hold of your life.

EVENING
Do you value time like gold and life itself? List some of the opportunities you had today. If a stranger were to evaluate how you used today's opportunities, how would you rate?

Make Time Your Servant

MORNING

One August, my digital watch stopped dead in its digits, and it took me a week to find a new battery. Six days without wearing a watch! You can't imagine the agony of it! Talk about Adam and Eve and their fig leaves! I never felt so naked in my life!

I'll bet you've experienced the same thing. It's a strange feeling to go without that watch around your wrist, isn't it? It's like going on a fast or quitting smoking. You set aside something you've grown dependent upon. You go "cold turkey," and you're not sure whether you're going to make it!

But, do you know what I discovered? After a day or two, you're free! No longer do you find yourself staring at your empty wrist or frantically dialing "time and temperature" every few seconds. It's as if you've entered a whole new world—a world where hours and minutes are unknown, and where the tyranny of the urgent is an ancient myth.

Jesus knew that world. Instinctively, he knew that time is meant to be our servant, not our master. We are so busy doing, we don't get to enjoy our lives—but not Jesus. We are so preoccupied with getting to tomorrow, we miss to-day—but Jesus didn't. Jesus took time to pray, time to enjoy his friends, time to help the needy. Yet, in three short years, he accomplished more than we could in a thousand lifetimes.

We jet from place to place; Jesus walked. We are slaves to the calendar; Jesus made it. He is its point of reference, with BC indicating what came before him, and AD indicating what has come since. There's a lesson in that—which only the great among us learn. When it's God who guides us, all we're meant to be and all we're meant to do come to pass in 24-hour days.

EVENING

How do you feel about your accomplishments today? Did you feel as though you were in control of your responsibilities, or as if they were in control of you? Name some specific changes which could improve the situation.

Take Time for Leisure

MORNING

Do you work more than sixty hours a week? Is the main subject of your conversation your work? When you're on vacation, do you feel you can't wait to get back on the job? If your answer's yes, chances are you're a compulsive worker—a workaholic.

As I write this, I'm nearing vacation time, and I must admit I like the idea. One reason why is I need time to get back in touch with myself and with God. But I haven't always felt that way. In the past I've been a compulsive worker, a time macho . . . one of those people the Russian author, Solzhenitsyn, describes as wasting themselves in senseless thrashing around for a handful of goods. They end up, he says, going to their graves without ever realizing their spiritual wealth.

But I'm reforming. When I go on vacation, I leave my brief case home. I take time for walks and for smelling flowers. I forget about racing through airports to catch planes. I forget about deadlines. I forget about feeling guilty for arriving late at unimportant meetings.

I've had to learn the hard way, and I'm still learning. But, now, at least, I've begun to grasp the truth that although it's wrong to waste time, it's equally wrong to crowd it too full. For example, look what the apostle Paul and John Bunyan and Aleksandr Solzhenitsyn were able to accomplish. Thanks to the enforced leisure of prison cells, they were able to write some of the world's greatest literature. If they had not found the solitude to get in touch with themselves and God, though, they never would have done it. That's why Bunyan prayed that God would keep him in prison until he finished his greatest work. The Bible says even Jesus required times for prayer and meditation; and if he did, we do, too.

EVENING

Do you take time to enjoy the fruits of your labor? Do you plan leisure activities every day? Do you take at least one day off in seven? When was the last time you had a vacation? Try to name five leisurely activities you enjoy which may be important to your health and well-being.

Use Your Moments as Responsibly as Your Hours

MORNING

Have you ever wondered how many marriages have broken down because the husband and wife didn't take time to communicate? Or how many drivers have died because they didn't take time to fasten their seat belts? Or how many heart attacks and strokes have occurred because people didn't have time for a checkup?

My friend and I pulled up to a gas station in the little town of York in Western Australia. I'd forgotten to fasten my seat belt, and the end of it was hanging out under the door. Pointing to it, the gas station attendant said, "You'd better be careful; that's police bait. You can get a stiff fine for not buckling up."

In Australia the law says you have to buckle your seat belt. I happen to believe it's a good law, even though I had neglected to buckle my own that day. But why hadn't I? Did I believe seat belts saved lives? Yes. Did I find seat belts uncomfortable and restricting in some way? No. Well, then, hadn't I had the time to get my belt fastened? As a matter of fact, I'd had all kinds of time.

That incident serves as a reminder to me that there are lots of important things we neglect that, attended to, would take only a tiny amount of our time. How much time does it take to fasten a seat belt? How much time does it take to send a thank-you note? How much time does it take to compliment our son or daughter or spouse? How much time does it take to plan a task well?

Actually, planning saves time in the end, and little sacrifices of time, like driving slower or getting a physical checkup, may save years of your life. For example, a recent study showed that just five minutes more time taken in driving would save 15,000 lives in a three-year period. And twenty minutes would save 35,000 lives.

The Bible teaches us to make the most of our time (Colossians 4:5); a part of that is using the least of our time wisely.

EVENING

Well, how did you do? Did you manage to capture some of those moments you might have wasted only yesterday? Did you manage to use the minutes as efficiently as the hours? Tomorrow, try taking some of your large projects and breaking them down into bite-size chunks. See if that doesn't help you still further.

Take Time for Those You Love

MORNING

I feel pretty smug right about now. I was just able to duck out of going to a committee meeting. One that, I am certain, didn't need me. You'll never guess what I did instead of going to that meeting. Something twice as important—something I plan to do a lot more of, too!

Instead of an hour with the committee, I spent an hour with my son, John. John is 15 months old. When I came in the front door, John spotted me and immediately picked up one of his picture books and led me to the couch.

"Whazzat?" he said, pointing to a strange-looking creature with a sidelong pickerel smile. "That's an alligator," I replied. "Whazzat?" he responded, this time pointing to a bear. And so it went from A to Z.

When I look at John, I am amazed. Yesterday he was a tiny baby; today he's a little boy. I realize how little time I'll have with him. After all, God's only loaned him to my wife and me for a few years.

There are two ways in which such precious time can slip through your fingers. One is unavoidable: life passes by too fast. But the other, you can do something about: *you* passing by life too fast! Believe me, you can get gobbled by committee meetings and urgent trivia if you're

121

not on your guard. You become a slave to clocks and calendars. You become paranoid about wasting time and, instead, time ends up wasting you.

I shall never forget the sad comment of a friend the other day. "I've got to go to court with my son, Mike," he said. "He's gotten into trouble again." Then, my friend's eyes filled with tears and he added, "You know, Mike's been living in our house 16 years now, but I've never really learned to know him."

That doesn't have to be you—take some time for something really important, *today*.

EVENING

What had priority on your agenda today? People? Or programs? How much time have you spent with your spouse? Your children? Those you love? Based on your performance today, which would you say comes first for you: calendars or people?

Get to Know God Better

Perspective

*"Let us draw near to God with a sincere heart in full
assurance of faith" (Hebrews 10:22).*

It is possible to know a great deal about God without
knowing him, to be informed about him without being
transformed by him. We know that because that was once
our position. Before we could know God we had to know
about God. But as with getting to know a friend, learning
to know God involves a constant cultivation of the relationship.

Christians don't always realize that. Often they think if
they read more books, hear more sermons, go to more Bible studies, and make Sunday school a priority, they will
get to know God better. But while all of those activities
are important, the way to really get to know God better is
to draw close to him.

Christians also tend to get so preoccupied with finding
biblical principles for overcoming defeat, making the
most of opportunities, learning to have a positive attitude,
and figuring out how to be happy all the time, they overlook the most important key to all those goals, and to having a great day every day—that of drawing close to God.
As J. I. Packer asks in his book, *Knowing God*, "What
were we made for? To know God. What aim should we
set ourselves in life? To know God. What is the 'eternal
life' that Jesus gives? Knowledge of God."

Let us turn our attention, then, to the seventh principle

for having a great day—the master key of drawing ever closer to God.

Be in Touch with God

"Only once have I been made mute," said Kahlil Gibran. "It was when a man asked me, 'Who are you?'"

"Who am I?" Do only poets and artists ask the question? And philosophers and theologians? No, all of us do.

When deep calls unto deep, we ask it. (That is how the Bible puts it in Psalm 42.) When we are soul-deep in trouble, or sorrow, or pain; when, by the towering grandeur of a snow-covered peak or by the meditative murmur of a purling brook, we are called beyond ourselves; when, through the majesty of the heavens or the miracle of birth, our eyes are opened with wonder, we ask, "Who am I?"

One of the psalms finds King David in such a mood. "As the deer pants for streams of water, so my soul pants for you, O God," he cries. Ruefully, he reflects on a former day when he would lead the procession to the house of God with joy and thanksgiving. But, now, God seems far away, and the deep in David cries out for something deep to answer it.

Pity the man or woman who has not experienced that. For the lack of deep calling out to deep betrays a shallowness of soul that sooner or later is smothered by the smallness of its world. In such a life our existence is taken lightly, and it is shallow calling unto shallow. There is no

127

stirring in the depths; no sense of needing to get in touch with God and oneself; no interest in the past or future; no roots, no wings—only this: a suffocating preoccupation with petty and temporary things.

What could be sadder? Or more tragic? To live out one's days without ever once having had a sense of who you are.

☀

EVENING

Have you lived today with a sense of destiny? Have you asked, "Who am I that thou art mindful of me?" Have you been in touch with God today?

Get to Know God Better

MORNING

There is only one sure way to have a sense of who you are. You must learn to know God better and better. As Vienna psychiatrist Viktor Frankl says, "There is in each of us a built-in urge to discover God, as real as the self-urge or the sex-urge." And until it is satisfied, life remains meaningless and shallow.

You need only listen to a man like the late French philosopher Albert Camus to know the truth of that: "To lose one's life is no great matter, but what's intolerable is to see one's life being drained of meaning, to be told there is no room for existing. A man cannot live without some reason for living."

Or listen to these thoughts of Ernest Hemingway, just months before a self-inflicted shotgun blast to the head ended an existence he felt to be meaningless: "What do you think happens to a man going on 62 when he realizes that he can never write the books or stories he promised himself; or do any of the other things he promised himself in the good old days?... If I can't exist on my own terms, then existence is impossible. Do you understand? That is how I've lived, and that is how I must live—or not live."

The emptiness that is felt by all such men is explained by a God-shaped vacuum in each of us. It is a deep thing, but some never learn that. They try to fill it with prosperity, popularity, position, prestige, pleasure, power, and a thousand other things. But none of those things is big enough. Only God can fill that empty place. Everything else rattles around in that hollow like a pebble in a dump truck.

So Frankl was right. Man's most basic need is the will-to-meaning, not the will-to-pleasure as Freud suggested, nor the will-to-power as Adler insisted. In those stirring moments when deep calls unto deep, only God answers satisfyingly and gives us an authentic sense of who we are.

EVENING

Have you allowed God to fill the empty places of your life? Has his fullness added satisfaction and meaning to your day? Have you worked at getting to know him better today?

Get to Know God
as Your Heavenly Father

MORNING

Who are you? The product of a chemical accident? Next of kin to vine-swinging apes? Somebody? Nobody? You don't know? I gave a friend of mine those options. Her answer was "none of the above." "Who are you, then?" I asked. "Why, I'm a child of God," she said.

My friend was right, of course. And you are actually and in fact a child of God, too—if you will be. Sin took away that privilege, but Jesus' death on the cross restored it. You say you don't understand how that could change things? Well, right now you don't need to. (There's plenty of time for that later on.) Right now all you need to do is believe God and claim your inheritance.

Then what? Well, if you're made in the image of God and have, by faith, become his child, then naturally, the more godlike you become, the more manlike (or womanlike) you will be. That's the way to be fully human, fully alive—the only way. That's the way to be all you were meant to be, to measure up to your full potential, to become all God had in mind when he first thought of you.

How do you do that—live that kind of life? You don't. You allow God to do it through you. That doesn't mean you don't put effort into it, nor does it mean it's not dif-

131

ficult, nor does it mean that you have a convenient excuse when you're not progressing toward your potential. What it does mean is this: relying on yourself is not enough. Rugged individualism, paving your own way, going it alone, or any other way you want to describe self-reliance just isn't enough. Only with God's help and guidance is there the prospect of making the most of your potential and gaining in the process a sense of who you are. Who's that? Why, a child of God, of course!

EVENING

Have you claimed your inheritance by placing your life in God's hands? Have you allowed him to lead you today, as a father leads his child?

Get to Know God's Plans for You

MORNING

What did God have in mind when he first thought of you? What possibilities did he plant within you? What uncultivated seedlings are there? That's important to discover, because unless we are working with God in the fulfillment of that potential, we can never be happy. Scatterbrained living is never happy living.

However, most people don't think that way. Most people have been hoodwinked into believing that the enjoyment of life depends upon external good fortune. But even when they have it and are still unhappy, they think that another path would bring them more success in their quest.

That's sad—in fact, tragic. Yet, the world is filled with such people—frustrated, inhibited, unorganized, half-made, unhappy individuals who are unable to put their lives together, because they haven't learned to ask the right questions.

When we find ourselves in that condition, we're prone to pin the blame on a number of things. We point to heredity and the circumstances of our upbringing. But thousands of people have risen above circumstances more hopeless than ours when they learned to ask the right question. Or we point to our present circumstances and powerlessness. But when we learn to ask the right question, we have the power of God at our disposal. And that's the greatest power in the universe. No, usually the only thing that gets in the way of becoming all we can be is ourselves. As Thoreau said, "As long as a man stands in his own way, everything else seems to be in his way."

Oh, the question! What is it? It is this: What does God want me to become? And according to the Gospel of John, if you do ask it, God will tell you.

EVENING

What do you think God had in mind when he first thought of you? Have you made any progress toward fulfilling that destiny today?

Remember You Are God's Creation

MORNING

I was wheeling my infant son through a department store while my wife tried on a dress. I met a friend, so I parked the stroller while we talked. A couple of moments later my little boy began cooing. We looked down and he was grinning from ear to ear. He had found a friend of his own.

My little John was looking into one of those floor-length mirrors that department stores scatter through their clothing sections. He was obviously delighted with what he saw.

I really can't tell you whether he had any sense of self as he viewed his reflection, but I hope he did. I hope, in some way, he could think to himself, "That's me, and I'm pleased."

I have a relative, though, who would not want me to say that. "Don't you remember Narcissus?" she'd be sure to ask.

"Isn't he the Greek movie star who fell in love with his image on the giant screen and turned up at every showing?"

She'd say, "No, it was a pool, not a movie screen, and he became so enchanted with his own reflection, he gazed at it till he pined away and died."

But I'd stick by my guns. I'd tell my dear aunt that, though I understand the danger of self-admiration, nevertheless, everyone of us needs to develop a sense of self-worth, because God has made us unique creations, in which he takes special pride. I'd tell her if we're supposed to love our neighbors as ourselves, then we first need to learn to love ourselves. As someone put it, "Self-disgust leads to self-rust; but self-esteem puts you on the beam!" As someone else put it, "God made you, and God don't make junk."

EVENING

Have you realized the difference between harmful pride and healthy self-esteem? Think of ten things you like about yourself. What would you like to add to the list? How can you go about it?

Ask God What He Wants You to Do

MORNING

What does God want from you? He made you, you know; and, obviously, it was for a purpose. What is that purpose? To know the answer to that question is to live a fulfilled life. To refuse to ask the question is to be forever unsatisfied. So, if you've never asked it, you need to. What *does* God have in mind for you? Does he want you to be an "A" student, a model housewife, a brilliant surgeon, a painter, an efficient factory worker?

The well-known minister Lloyd Olgive was confronted with that question a while back, and the answer surprised him. At the end of a very difficult week, a friend approached him and said, "Lloyd, I want your life to be as beautiful as it was in the mind of God when he first thought of you." What a liberating suggestion! But what was in the mind of God when he first thought of Lloyd Olgive? Lloyd gave much thought to it. What did God want his human existence to be like? He prayed about it. He waited for an answer. Then, God seemed to say to him, "Christ, Lloyd, Jesus Christ! That's how I first thought of you."

The apostle Paul came to the same conclusion. He says, God "chose us ... before the creation of the world to be holy and blameless in his sight" (Ephesians 1:4, NIV).

137

That's what God had in mind. Not that we should be an effective or efficient this or that, but that through Jesus Christ, we should be like Jesus Christ: holy and blameless. What a wonderful plan! What better blueprint for any of our lives could God have come up with?

Are you seeking more and more to live a Christlike life? How did you do today?

Fix Your Mind on God

MORNING

Do you ever get the feeling there are two of you—one that wants you to do right and one that wants to pull you down—so that you feel torn, unable to find direction? Or restless and ill at ease about what you're doing with your life—like you're measuring it out with coffee spoons?

Do you remember Stephen Leacock's famous rider who "flung himself upon his horse and rode madly off in all directions?" That is a perfect picture of us sometimes, isn't it? We feel pulled in a dozen different directions from the outside and within. We live as restlessly as the teenagers who circle drive-in restaurants. We think of the Bible verse that says, "We labor and have no rest" (Lamentations 5:5) or the one that describes those who are like the troubled sea, when it cannot rest (Isaiah 57:20).

But the same book of the Bible in which that verse is found also has this to say: "Thou wilt keep him in perfect peace, whose mind is stayed on thee" (Isaiah 26:3, KJV). Is it true? Can Christ really do that for you? Listen to the words of singer B. J. Thomas from his book, *Home Where I Belong:*

"I'm into my third year as a Christian now, and I never realized how beautiful life could be. I have new resources and perspectives for dealing with the little irritations (and the big ones) that come along."

139

Those new resources for peaceful living are available to you, too, because *Jesus* is available. God brings that fragmented feeling to an end once we realize, as B. J. Thomas did, that real peace—perfect peace—is essentially a state of going somewhere—wholeheartedly, one-directionally—with our mind fixed on him.

EVENING
Is your mind fixed on God? What evidence was there of it as you went about your tasks today?

WEEK 8

Learn the Habit of Daily Prayer

Perspective

*"And pray in the Spirit on all occasions with all kinds
of prayers and requests" (Ephesians 6:18).*

Perhaps the best way to learn to know God better is
through prayer. Paul S. Rees once said, "If we are willing
to take hours on end to learn to play a piano, or operate a
computer, or fly an airplane, it is sheer nonsense for us to
imagine that we can learn the high art of getting
guidance through communion with the Lord without being willing to set aside time for it. It is no accident that
the Bible speaks of prayer as a form of waiting on God."
Deep down, I think that's something we all know. But the
gap between that knowledge and practicing it is hard to
bridge.

In this final week of understanding some of the principles that help make ordinary days extraordinary ones, I
can think of no better focus than considering ways to
make prayer a more important event in our lives. As we
shall be reminded, the very reason why Christ died on the
cross was that we might have access to God. But we must
find a way to move from that knowledge of the importance of prayer to the actual implementation of the
kind of prayer Paul urges us to offer in the passage quoted
above.

My prayer is that you will make significant progress in
that pursuit this week and in the weeks ahead, and so
move even further along on your way to having great
days every day.

Make Prayer a Priority

MORNING

A famous American once said: "The spectacle of a nation praying is more awe-inspiring than the explosion of an atomic bomb. The force of prayer is greater than any possible combination of man-made powers, because prayer is man's greatest means of tapping the resources of God."

Occasionally I see books with titles like *The Power of Prayer*. But really it's the power of God they're talking about. Prayer is simply the channel of communication we have with God, through which his power is available. That's good news, but it's also sad news. For even though we can come to God and pray to God and lay hold of this tremendous power, few people do. Most people come to God only in emergencies. Prayer is simply not a priority in their lives.

Someone asked Emily Post, "What's the correct response when you're invited to the White House, and you have a previous engagement?" Her answer was, "An invitation to dinner at the White House is a command, and automatically cancels all other engagements." Shouldn't that be our view of prayer, too? Each of us should have a daily engagement—that takes priority over everything else in our calendar—to learn the will and way of God and to receive his help and strength through prayer.

If we come to God in such a way, seeking to hear him and to do his will, we will never be disappointed. We never have to be afraid that God won't hear us. Or that God won't receive us. We can come to him as our Father, and he will talk back to us as his children.

EVENING

If you have followed this book faithfully the last seven weeks, no doubt prayer has already become a larger priority for you. How can you make it an even deeper experience?

Make Prayer a Habit

I read about a little girl named Suzanne. She ended a prayer one evening like this: "Good-bye, dear Lord, we're moving to New York. It's really been nice knowing you though. Amen."

Now many of us pray more like little Suzanne than we care to admit. Like this little girl, we pray as though God were only in certain places, but it's not in New York that we look for him. It's wherever we get into trouble.

Praying of that sort is called foxhole praying by some. It describes a pattern of praying in which we come to God only in our moments of desperation. And it describes an attitude toward God which is not indicative of real trust, but of looking to God as a kind of last resort. Out of desperation we call on God just in case there is a God, and just in case he really cares. There is no relationship, no real reliance either. We are open to use God but not open for him to use us.

But the Bible says we should pray unceasingly, and it says that because God is interested in every moment of our lives and not just the crisis moments. So prayer is not just a hot line to heaven, but an open channel of communication. Prayer is, in other words, being intimate with God.

Someone has said, "Hem in the day with prayer and it

will be less likely to ravel out before night." I like that. And prayer is so simple; it is like quietly opening a door, slipping into the very presence of God, and carrying on a conversation with a friend.

So why not resolve to make prayer a habit rather than a last resort? Not only will you find God more ready to answer your prayers, but you'll find him ready to take the desperateness out of your troubles even before you've asked, for it's pretty hard to get swept off your feet when you're already on your knees.

EVENING

Reread Psalm 55:16, 17. Is prayer a habit for you? But habits can become routine. How do you keep your prayer from deadness and dullness, therefore?

Use the Lord's Prayer as Your Pattern

MORNING

When Jesus walked the shores of Lake Galilee, his disciples asked him, "Lord, teach us to pray" (Luke 11:1). Many of us feel that need, too. We want to grow in our ability to communicate with God, because we've learned—when we've truly been in touch with ourselves—that our life isn't complete without his presence.

When we're truly in touch with ourselves, we recognize that we are not pure intellect, pure emotion, or mere physical beings. We have a spiritual side, too. So, just as it would be silly for us not to eat, it is silly not to pray. As Jesus said one time, "Man does not live by bread alone" (Matthew 4:4). Because we are spiritual beings, there is an innate longing in each of us to be in touch with God.

Now when we recognize that, we also become aware of the need to learn to pray. In a large city church, a priest observed a certain man who came daily, knelt for only a moment, and then was on his way. One day the priest had a chance to talk with him. He asked, "When you kneel down so briefly, what do you say?" The man replied, "When I come here at noon, I simply say, 'Jesus, this is Jimmy.'" There's something beautiful about a simple prayer like that, but most of us would not be satisfied to stop there. We want to grow in our prayer lives.

We want to know what to ask God for, and how to ask it. Prayer is no longer a panic button for us; and we've gotten beyond prayer as a mere "hello." So how do we grow in our ability to communicate with God?

The simplest answer is to use the prayer Jesus taught his disciples as a model, which is what he intended. Jesus taught it, not for repetition, but as a pattern. It contains all the ingredients of a mature prayer to God.

EVENING

Pray the Lord's Prayer a phrase at a time. Amplify each phrase with ascriptions of praise, specific requests, and thanksgiving.

Pray with Expectancy

MORNING

Somewhere I read that many a fellow praying for rain has his tub the wrong side up. For me, reading that was like looking in a mirror. For as I look back on the requests I've made to God over the years, if I'm honest, I have to admit that many times I asked without really expecting an answer.

There's an interesting story in the Bible about a group of people who were praying for the release of the apostle Peter. Peter had been imprisoned by the authorities, and his life was in danger. In response to the requests of these people, God sent an angel to Peter's cell who released Peter's shackles, opened the door of the cell, and led Peter outside the prison gates to safety.

Now the first thing Peter did was to go to the very house where this little prayer meeting was going on. They were praying upstairs and a little girl named Rhoda came down to the front door when Peter began to knock. Immediately she recognized it was Peter, but she became so excited, she forgot to open the door and flew back up the stairs to tell everyone that their prayers for Peter had been answered. But what do you suppose their response was? Did they shout "hallelujah?" No, they said to this little girl, "You're crazy."

But the little girl kept insisting that it really was Peter,

151

and she seemed so convinced they came up with another answer. They said to her, "Well, it must be his angel."

Now what was happening was this. These folks were praying for Peter's deliverance, but they really didn't expect God to answer their prayers.

The Bible points out again and again that faith is essential to answered prayer. In this case, God answered their prayers even though their faith was lacking. But because God wants us to learn to trust him, he often does not answer "yes" until we become really serious and make our requests expectantly.

☀

EVENING

What were your requests of God today? Did you pray with expectation? Do you believe God will answer those requests? Read Matthew 7:9-11.

Believe That God Knows Best

MORNING

I keep a little notebook in which I record my prayer requests. After each request are three columns. The first column has the heading "yes," the second "wait," and the third "no." And you'd be surprised at how many times the Lord answers my prayers "no."

To be sure, there are many more "yeses" to my prayer requests than "no." But there have been many "nos," and I'd like to share with you some of the reasons why. One reason is summed up in a statement of Jesus. "You do not understand what you are asking," he said (Matthew 20:22, NEB). In other words, a lot of times we ask God for something unwisely, not realizing that if God were to answer our request "yes," the granting of that request would be more harmful to us than beneficial.

A student pilot was asked by her instructor to turn over the controls. The student protested, "I know how to land the plane. I've landed it before, let me do it now." The instructor replied, "No, I'm sorry, you can't land the plane. I realize you've done it before, but you're not experienced enough to land in these crosswinds."

Monica, the mother of St. Augustine, prayed all one night that God wouldn't let her son sail for Italy. She felt all hope for his becoming a Christian would be gone if he did. But while she was still praying, her son sailed. What Monica didn't realize was that it was in Italy that her son, Augustine, would meet God. So, although God said "no" to Monica's request, he was saying no to the form of it, not the substance of it. He said "no" to what she asked, but "yes" to what she desired.

So when God answers no to our requests, we need to learn to accept it. He is always looking out for our good, even though it is not always possible for us to understand it in the crisis of the moment.

EVENING

How has God answered some of your recent requests? Has today's meditation shed light on any confusing answer you've received? How?

Be Willing to Wait

MORNING

God answers our prayers one of three ways: "yes," "no," and "wait." Often, however, we interpret his answer as "no" when he is really saying "wait." That points to the importance of patience in praying—which has a bitter taste for the moment, but produces sweet fruit in the end.

Jesus spoke a parable one time in order to show his listeners that they should keep on praying and never lose heart. He said, "There was once a judge who cared nothing for God or man, and in the same town there was a widow who constantly came before him demanding justice against her opponent. For a long time he refused; but in the end he said to himself, 'True, I care nothing for God or man, but this widow is so great a nuisance that I will see her righted before she wears me out with her persistence.' "

Now, of course, Jesus' point was not that God wears out with persistence. Jesus' point was even as he said: "When God's answer seems to be no, we should not lose heart, because he may only be saying wait."

Sometimes God says wait because we are not ready to receive the things we ask for. Sometimes he says wait because the conditions aren't just right. Sometimes he says wait because he wants to show us a better option, and yet he gives us the choice between the two. But whatever the reason, it is always for our own good.

I have the feeling, though, the main reason why God says wait is to teach us patience and trust. When we have to wait on God, we necessarily learn dependence in the process of waiting.

So don't be like the little girl who, after several hours of fishing, threw her pole down and cried, "I quit."

"What's the matter?" her father asked.

"Nothing," said the girl. "Except I can't seem to get waited on."

When you make your requests known to God and you can't seem to get waited on, just wait on. When you are patient, the answer is sure to come.

EVENING

Read Luke 11:6-8. Have you learned to be persistent, yet patient in making your requests known to God? Can you think of answers to prayer which were received only after a long wait?

Be Willing to Be God's Answer

MORNING

"Prayer is not conquering God's reluctance, but laying hold of God's willingness," someone has said. But if you've had very much experience at all in prayer, you have noticed as I have that oftentimes God is very unwilling.

Recently I was reading an article by the well-known Christian writer William Barclay. He was talking about prayer, and he pointed out that prayer is not merely dumping our problems into God's lap, but asking God to give us the strength and wisdom to work at the problems we face. I needed to be reminded of that, because often I find myself doing just what Barclay says we shouldn't do. It's easy to forget that God has given us a brain and arms and legs for a reason. Sure, he wants us to pray, but he also wants us to think and work. Just as the parts of the body work together, so thinking and working and praying must work together.

Whenever our family goes somewhere which involves driving for a considerable distance, we take the time to pray for safety before we leave our house. But suppose after praying, I were simply to push the cruise control button in our car, recline the seat, and go to sleep—could we really expect to arrive at our destination safely? Of

157

course not. For my praying must, in that instance, be accompanied by thinking.

Likewise, many prayers are answered only when we combine our requests with the willingness to work. The preacher who continually climbs into his pulpit without any preparation or forethought cannot expect to preach effective sermons week after week. God's inspiration comes not only in the moment, but in the hard work of preparation as well. That is why Charles Spurgeon once said, "Pray to God, but keep the hammer going."

So next time you question whether God is doing his part in answer to a prayer request, why not first ask, "Am I doing my part?"

EVENING

How have you sought to be part of God's anwer to your own recent requests? How are you working at it right now?

The Author

Arthur G. McPhee is a pastor, teacher, and writer from Needham Heights, Massachusetts. His books include *Friendship Evangelism* and *Traveling Light*. He has lectured at numerous colleges and seminaries, and serves as an adjunct instructor at Eastern Mennonite Seminary in Harrisonburg, Virginia.

Persons from hundreds of churches have participated in McPhee's seminars on relational evangelism and church growth dynamics. He has also been radio speaker on *The Mennonite Hour* and on *Art McPhee in Touch*.

Born in Claremont, New Hampshire, Art was ordained to the Christian ministry in 1971 while pastor of the Stahl Mennonite Church in Johnstown, Pennsylvania. From 1973 to 1981, he pastored Lindale Mennonite Church in Linville, Virginia. Presently, he serves the newly formed Good Shepherd Christian Fellowship near Boston, Massachusetts.

Arthur and Evelyn (Horst) McPhee are the parents of a son, John.

DATE DUE

NOV 2 6 1984			
DEC 1 3 1984			
JAN 2 9 1985			
12/16/85			
SEP 2 6 1988			

HIGHSMITH 45-102   PRINTED IN U.S.A.